Practical Oracle JET

Developing Enterprise Applications in JavaScript

Daniel Curtis

Practical Oracle JET: Developing Enterprise Applications in JavaScript

Daniel Curtis
Birmingham, UK

ISBN-13 (pbk): 978-1-4842-4345-9   ISBN-13 (electronic): 978-1-4842-4346-6
https://doi.org/10.1007/978-1-4842-4346-6

Library of Congress Control Number: 2019935824

Managing Director, Apress Media LLC: Welmoed Spahr
Acquisitions Editor: Jonathan Gennick
Development Editor: Laura Berendson
Coordinating Editor: Jill Balzano

Cover image designed by Freepik (www.freepik.com)

Distributed to the book trade worldwide by Springer Science+Business Media New York, 233 Spring Street, 6th Floor, New York, NY 10013. Phone 1-800-SPRINGER, fax (201) 348-4505, e-mail orders-ny@springer-sbm.com, or visit www.springeronline.com. Apress Media, LLC is a California LLC and the sole member (owner) is Springer Science+Business Media Finance Inc (SSBM Finance Inc). SSBM Finance Inc is a **Delaware** corporation.

For information on translations, please e-mail rights@apress.com, or visit www.apress.com/rights-permissions.

Apress titles may be purchased in bulk for academic, corporate, or promotional use. eBook versions and licenses are also available for most titles. For more information, reference our Print and eBook Bulk Sales web page at www.apress.com/bulk-sales.

Any source code or other supplementary material referenced by the author in this book is available to readers on GitHub via the book's product page, located at www.apress.com/9781484243459. For more detailed information, please visit www.apress.com/source-code.

Printed on acid-free paper

Dedicated to all my family, friends, and Charlotte.
To Berni, your spirit and determination continue to influence us all.

Table of Contents

About the Author

 **Daniel Curtis** is a front-end developer specializing in Oracle's JavaScript Extension Toolkit (JET). He has had an interest in technology from an early age, particularly web development, for which he taught himself PHP, MySQL, and HTML back in 2008. This eventually led him to build web sites for customers, alongside his studies throughout A levels and university.

Since graduating, he now has more than five years' experience working with different Oracle front-end technologies, including Oracle's Application Development Framework (ADF), WebCenter Portal, and WebCenter Sites. He works for Griffiths Waite, a company based in Birmingham, UK, developing solutions for a number of enterprise customers. Daniel has most recently been involved in modernizing applications in Oracle JET and has written articles on the technology for Medium, the Oracle developer publication.

About the Technical Reviewer

Geertjan Wielenga is an open source enthusiast working at Oracle and, before that, Sun Microsystems. Since starting at Sun Microsystems in Prague, Czech Republic, in 2004, he has primarily focused on writing documentation and training materials for the free and open source NetBeans IDE. Gradually, as he participated in conferences and began setting up workshops, especially on the use of NetBeans IDE for the development of Java applications, as well as introductions to the NetBeans APIs and the development of large Java Swing desktop applications on top of the NetBeans platform, he grew into a developer advocacy and product management role and specialized in Java and the tooling requirements connected to NetBeans IDE in support of Java.

When Oracle took over Sun Microsystems, and the developer ecosystem began to embrace JavaScript as a useful language and ecosystem for the development of enterprise applications, NetBeans IDE was repositioned to provide tooling for JavaScript as much as it had for Java. Oracle's strategy for JavaScript was developed and expanded over the years into an in-house front-end technology stack called Oracle JET. When Oracle JET was made available for external use as a free and open source technology stack, Geertjan joined the related product management team at Oracle, focusing specifically on promoting Oracle JET to the Oracle ecosystem and beyond.

In the meantime, Oracle decided to share the cost of ownership of NetBeans IDE and, accordingly, donated it to the Apache Software Foundation. Together with his focus on promoting Oracle JET, Geertjan has been leading the NetBeans IDE transition of NetBeans IDE to the Apache Software Foundation from within Oracle.

Through his experiences with customers, partners, and conferences, Geertjan has seen the strengths of the JavaScript ecosystem, as well as its gaps in the enterprise ecosystem. He has seen time and again how enterprises value Oracle JET's enterprise-grade features and functionalities, and this continues to enthuse him in his role as product manager for Oracle JET.

Acknowledgments

I would like to thank everyone who has been involved in the journey of putting this project together. A special thank you to my colleagues at Griffiths Waite for their support and guidance from the get-go, especially to Andrew Bennett and Rich Barber.

Thank you to my amazing girlfriend, Charlotte, who has not only had to put up with the late nights of writing but also created the book illustrations and given much needed encouragement along the way.

To my parents and family, thank you so much for your support always.

Finally, a thank you to Nick Dobson, for pushing me to do this; to Ian Watson, for proofreading; and to Reece Jacques, Oliver Butler, and James Potts, for being the best support network anyone could ask for.

Introduction

Practical Oracle JET will walk you through the process of developing a functional application, using Oracle's JavaScript Extension Toolkit (JET). Rather than being a typical theoretical book, it will guide you through the practical creation of a complete support ticket system, using a variety of different components bundled with the toolkit, including lists, inputs, and visualizations. The skills acquired from reading this book and working the examples will equip you to build your own applications and take your understanding even further to more advanced topics.

A basic knowledge of JavaScript is expected before proceeding with this book. The technologies that JET uses under the hood will be explored, and complete code will be given in a chapter-by-chapter format on GitHub or JSFiddle (where specified).

CHAPTER 1

User Experience in Enterprise Applications

User experience is a term often used when developing any kind of web interface. Such an interface could be for a web site or web application. Implementing user experience essentially requires getting the right balance between the end goals of the business, technical restraints, and preferences of end users. User experience involves much more than just reducing the amount of clicks a user takes to achieve a goal. A lot of factors are considered in getting it right.

A report conducted by Nielsen indicated that intranet (enterprise) users are stuck at a low level of productivity, and the average employee success rate at basic intranet tasks decreased over time. Web sites were said to have a much higher success rate. Why is this?

Enterprise systems can be very complicated, and often, a lot of different functionality can be required in a single system. Imagine an application for a mortgage broker that processes mortgage applications. Applying for a mortgage is complicated in itself when you are one buyer dealing with one bank. Imagine designing an interface that has to integrate with 30 different banks. Each one of these banks may have different data required in different formats, so you could end up having to design 30 different user-interface forms to achieve the same requirement within a single application. If we throw in different levels of user access, so that different people can work on different parts of the application, you can see how quickly it can become complex and potentially cause usability issues.

As the design becomes more complicated, the development can too, leading to functionality challenges. With tight deadlines it is possible to end up with a scenario in which the design and user experience analysis takes a back seat to getting the business functionality delivered. This is a common scenario, illustrated in Figure 1-1, and results in applications that may achieve the functionality set out in the requirements

1

© Daniel Curtis 2019
D. Curtis, *Practical Oracle JET*, https://doi.org/10.1007/978-1-4842-4346-6_1

but may not be the most usable. When this occurs, and end users are logging on to the application day in and day out, the experience for the user becomes unpleasant and ultimately, lowers productivity.

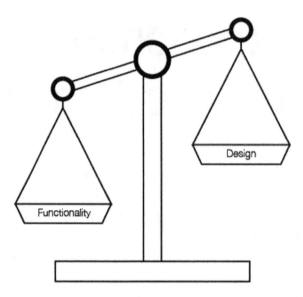

Figure 1-1. *Functionality outweighing design*

Tie any complexity in with the fact that enterprise application solutions are typically quite behind the latest trends (preferring stability over latest versions), and it begins to become obvious why web sites are more likely to be successful, as they can implement the latest usability guidelines and functionality provided by the toolkits they are using.

Technology Architecture Limitations

There was once a time when server-side rendering of web sites did exactly what it needed to. There was little interaction required between the client and server, other than requesting a URL and being returned a static HTML page with text and images. Today this is no longer the case, as web sites are now more like applications but are still behaving (from a technology perspective) like traditional web sites.

With server-side web applications, a web browser must make a request to the server and await a response, in order to complete a task that a user has requested. This task could be a request for data, or it could be something as simple as opening a pop-up window. The latency of the round-trip to the server, as illustrated in Figure 1-2, could have detrimental effects on usability. Even a small delay can be a nuisance when someone is using a system for day-to-day tasks.

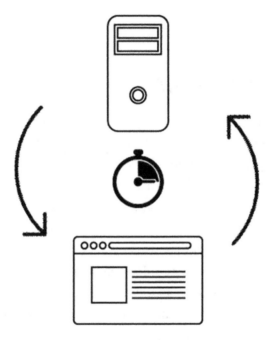

Figure 1-2. *Round-trips to a server can take time*

Long-running tasks, for which the browser is awaiting the response from the server can cause usability headaches. A data export may lock the UI functionality until the server has completed the task, and long batch jobs that take hours can leave a user without being able to use an application at all.

 A lot of existing enterprise applications have been developed with the traditional server-side rendering, and more recently the sort of problems I've just described have caused a rethink in the way that web technologies are being developed. As web browsers have become more powerful and are able to handle more complicated calculations, client-side frameworks are starting to become more popular. The server becomes responsible only for serving the main application file on initial load, subsequent module loading and API calls for data. The client therefore is responsible for processing and running the code locally.

The benefits of this kind of architecture are massive for enterprise applications, the speed of interactivity being most noticeable, but also the scalability. Servers no longer have to be monolithic to handle the processing of hundreds or thousands of concurrent users.

This leads me to believe that we are at a point of transformation in the enterprise industry. With client-side toolkits becoming increasingly popular, and cloud computing becoming more mature, we may finally be at the cornerstone of building really great enterprise solutions.

Closed Source Usability

Closed source systems, in which a developer does not have direct access to view or modify the source code of the framework being used, can have an indirect impact on the usability of an application. Although these kinds of frameworks have many benefits, such as rapid development and enterprise support, they force the developer to use the components and technology that the framework provides. These components will have been trialed and tested against common business use cases; however, real-life use cases may have differing requirements that are not supported.

Even the smallest unsupported requirement can have a huge impact on time lines, as a developer struggles to "fight against the framework" to achieve the desired outcome. If this is not possible, an alternative may be presented that still achieves the desired functionality, at the cost of the user experience.

Ideally, we want a toolkit that completely eliminates any struggle against framework components. Developers shouldn't be restricted by the tools they are using. They should be able to pull from the open source community and have a multitude of different options available.

Improving Usability

Enterprise applications should be more successful than web sites, as designers will have a smaller subset of users to design for, and have easier access to usability data, resulting in a product for which the requirements have been thought out more efficiently.
Part (but not all) of the problem is owing to the technology choices that are made for enterprise applications. By addressing the following points, some fundamental usability issues can be prevented.

Client-side framework: Move away from the traditional client-server model. Choose a technology that runs the application on the client, mitigating the need for a round-trip to the server every time a change occurs on the page.

> By running the application on the client, it opens up the potential for a faster, fluid, and more responsive experience for users, in addition to a multitude of other benefits that will be explored during the course of this book.

Designer/developer harmony: Choose a toolkit that already has some design guidelines in place (and can be easily extended), so that designers have clear visibility of the toolkit's components and capabilities. Ideally, the toolkit should help to close the gap between design and development teams.

Open source: Development teams should have the ability and freedom to customize code to achieve the desired requirements outlined by both the business and design experts. Developers should also benefit from being able to harness the ever-expanding sea of component libraries available and customize any component libraries included within the vendor toolkit.

Keeping up with trends: Enterprise frameworks can often be quite behind the latest trends, to ensure they have stability, and upgrading can sometimes be an expensive task. The issue then is that user-interface trends change very quickly, so systems can become outdated before they are even launched. Ideally, it is best to get a good balance between stability and newer features, without the need to have monolithic yearly upgrades that take ages to implement and are still way behind the latest technologies. Smaller, incremental upgrades throughout the year can help with this.

Summary

This book is not about how we should visually design an application. (There are plenty of other books that cover the best practices for that.) It is more of a means of highlighting the issues with enterprise applications and how you, as a developer, can use a toolkit that will provide the necessary components to develop great applications with the least effort possible required for design thought. Although, as a developer it is good to consider design, the basic UX principles should be provided to you by the tools that you are using.

In addition, we want a set of tools that will aid designers and developers to work side by side seamlessly. It is becoming clearer that there is more of an overlap between a "UX designer" and a "front-end developer," with UX designers being able not only to design an interface but also to implement the basic CSS and HTML markup for the page, with a developer coming in afterward and hooking up all the back-end business logic.

CHAPTER 2

Oracle JET As a Solution

There may finally be a solution to developing great enterprise applications—solutions that are both functionally rich and beautiful in design. For the past four years, Oracle JavaScript Extension Toolkit (JET) has been used for many internal Oracle applications. In fact, a lot of the Oracle Cloud Services are being built using Oracle JET. VBCS (Visual Builder Cloud Service) is an Oracle SaaS product that is built on top of JET and gives users the ability to declaratively build rich applications in no time at all.

There is often an anxiety that surrounds the JavaScript ecosystem, and quite rightly so. The libraries and trends are changing so rapidly that it is becoming increasingly difficult for developers to keep up and for enterprise customers to trust that the software they are investing in will be relevant a few months later. With Oracle JET, developers have access to a modern JavaScript toolkit that challenges the frameworks of the past by offering rapid development, extensibility, and the stability and support that you come to expect from Oracle.

JET is essentially a group of different JavaScript libraries and build tools, pulled together into a toolkit. Some of these libraries are open source and commonly known, such as JQuery, RequireJS, and KnockoutJS. There are also libraries that are built by Oracle but still are open source, such as the feature-rich Oracle JET visualization components that come with years of maturity inherited from Oracle ADF and WebCenter products.

In this chapter, you are going to explore some of the libraries that make up the JET toolkit, and by the end, you should have a good understanding of the core technologies you need to be aware of before we move on to using them within an Oracle JET project.

All examples throughout this chapter are hosted on JSFiddle, so you can use and extend the examples yourself. Try not to worry too much about how these examples are set up. Later in the book you will see how to set up a JET application. For now, just concentrate on the concepts and technologies that JET uses.

© Daniel Curtis 2019
D. Curtis, *Practical Oracle JET*, https://doi.org/10.1007/978-1-4842-4346-6_2

RequireJS

RequireJS is a JavaScript library that is used for loading in JavaScript files. It implements a specification called AMD, which stands for *Asynchronous Module Definition*.

Normally, when including multiple JavaScript libraries, an HTML file would include a bunch of script tags similar to the following:

```
<script src="jQuery.js"></script>
<script src="library1.js"></script>
<script src="library2.js"></script>
<script src="library3.js"></script>
```

Loading libraries in this way isn't an issue when there are only a few libraries to include, but it can become a real problem when there are a large number of JavaScript files, as it can be a nightmare to manage and also requires a request for each and every library upon page load.

Dependencies can be an issue too. If a library is dependent on another that has not been loaded yet, it will cause an error. (It is possible that you have seen the "$ is undefined" error once or twice.)

If we change the import order of the script tags to place jQuery at the bottom, and the libraries are dependent on jQuery, the application will throw errors.

```
<script src="library1.js"></script>
<script src="library2.js"></script>
<script src="library3.js"></script>
<script src="jQuery.js"></script>
```

RequireJS solves the preceding problems, as it takes care of loading in the JavaScript libraries and ensures that they are loaded in the correct order and when they are needed. In order to understand how this works, we must first take a look at the AMD specification.

The AMD specification outlines a single function, called define, which looks like this:

```
define(id?, dependencies?, factory);
```

There are three arguments to the define function, and these are as follows:

- id: This is the id for the module that is being defined. The id argument is optional, and we won't really be using it in the context of JET.

- dependencies: This is an array of JavaScript libraries that must be loaded for the factory to run.

- factory: This is the code that will be running once all the dependencies are loaded.

So, with the AMD definition, you are able to set an identifier for the define block, include all the dependencies, and then finally run a module of code that uses the dependencies that have been defined. Next, we will take a look at a RequireJS example, using the define block.

define Example

The define syntax in RequireJS is fairly straightforward, and by applying the AMD define function, we can write the following:

```
define(['jquery', 'myLibrary'], function($) {
  // Application code logic here
});
```

The argument that is passed into the factory function ($) will reference the corresponding library from the dependency list. In this case, it will be used to reference jQuery, as it is the first item in the dependency list. You should not always have to pass the library into your factory function, as we have done with jQuery. It is only required when the library returns an object that you must use. In this scenario, myLibrary does not return anything, and, therefore, it does not require a corresponding argument within the function.

However, if myLibrary did have a return value, you would add another argument into the function, as in the following:

```
define(['jquery', 'myLibrary'], function($, myLib) {
  // Application code logic here
});
```

Ordering is important here. Although define will take care of JavaScript loading dependencies, the order of the arguments into the function matters. Swapping the dependency ordering can cause mapping inconsistencies.

```
define(['myLibrary', 'jquery'], function($, myLib) {
  // Application code logic here
});
```

In the preceding example, using $ will map to myLibrary instead of jquery. Therefore, it is important to make sure the mapping is correct and that all dependencies that have a return value are placed at the start of the dependency list.

Under the Hood of RequireJS

RequireJS takes the dependency list you specify, works out the correct ordering, and then adds the script tags into the head of the page dynamically. Figures 2-1 and 2-2 visualise this process in practice. Figure 2-1 shows the block skeleton, and Figure 2-2 shows the resulting HTML script tags.

```
1    define(['jquery', 'library1', 'library2', 'library3'], function ($) {
2
3    });|
```

Figure 2-1. *Define block skeleton with dependencies*

```html
<!DOCTYPE html>
▼ <html>
  ▼ <head>
      <title>Example require</title>
      <script data-main="js/app" src="js/libs/require.js"></script>
      <script type="text/javascript" charset="utf-8" async data-
      requirecontext="_" data-requiremodule="app" src="js/
      app.js"></script>
      <script type="text/javascript" charset="utf-8" async data-
      requirecontext="_" data-requiremodule="app/main" src="js/libs/
      ../app/main.js"></script>
      <script type="text/javascript" charset="utf-8" async data-
      requirecontext="_" data-requiremodule="jquery" src="js/libs/
      jquery.js"></script>
      <script type="text/javascript" charset="utf-8" async data-
      requirecontext="_" data-requiremodule="library1" src="js/libs/
      library1.js"></script>
      <script type="text/javascript" charset="utf-8" async data-
      requirecontext="_" data-requiremodule="library2" src="js/libs/
      library2.js"></script>
      <script type="text/javascript" charset="utf-8" async data-
      requirecontext="_" data-requiremodule="library3" src="js/libs/
      library3.js"></script>
    </head>
    <body> </body> = $0
  </html>
```

Figure 2-2. `index.html` *file with script tags added into the DOM*

require vs. define

We have looked into the define function, but RequireJS also has a function called require. It is possible to use both the require and define functions within RequireJS. As a rule of thumb, require should be used to run immediate functionalities, and define should be used to define modules of code that can be used in multiple locations within an application.

In modular applications, this will result in a single require block to load in all the immediate application logic that is necessary for the application to initialize and run, followed by multiple define blocks used across the application for individual modules of code.

Using RequireJS in JET

Now that you understand what problems RequireJS solves, let's take a look at how it is implemented within an Oracle JET application. RequireJS is included out of the box when you scaffold your JET application, and the following is added at the bottom of the index.html file of a new project:

```
<script type="text/javascript" src="js/libs/require/require.js"></script>
<script type="text/javascript" src="js/main.js"></script>
```

The main.js file is an important piece of the RequireJS puzzle that comes bundled with a JET application. The file contains a list of all the library dependencies required for the project to run (also known as the configuration block). It will also include a require block, which loads all the libraries required to kick-start the JET application. It is essentially an entry point into your application code.

Configuration

Within the main.js file, you will have what is called the "configuration block." The configuration essentially sets the base location (baseUrl) of the JavaScript modules and declares all the libraries that the application will be using.

The example in Listing 2-1 is the configuration block and lists some of the default libraries that are required to run JET. Later in the book, we will be adding new libraries to the paths object.

Listing 2-1. Example of a Configuration Block

```
requirejs.config(
{
  baseUrl: 'js',

  // Path mappings for the logical module names
  // Update the main-release-paths.json for release mode when updating the
  mappings
  paths:
  //injector:mainReleasePaths
  {
     'knockout': 'libs/knockout/knockout-3.4.2.debug',
     'jquery': 'libs/jquery/jquery-3.3.1',
     'jqueryui-amd': 'libs/jquery/jqueryui-amd-1.12.1',
     'promise': 'libs/es6-promise/es6-promise',
     'hammerjs': 'libs/hammer/hammer-2.0.8',
     'ojdnd': 'libs/dnd-polyfill/dnd-polyfill-1.0.0',
     'ojs': 'libs/oj/v6.0.0/debug',
     'ojL10n': 'libs/oj/v6.0.0/ojL10n',
     'ojtranslations': 'libs/oj/v6.0.0/resources',
     'text': 'libs/require/text',
     'signals': 'libs/js-signals/signals',
     'customElements': 'libs/webcomponents/custom-elements.min',
     'proj4': 'libs/proj4js/dist/proj4-src',
     'css': 'libs/require-css/css',
  }
  //endinjector

  ,
  // Shim configurations for modules that do not expose AMD
  shim:
  {
```

```
    'jquery':
    {
      exports: ['jQuery', '$']
    }
  }
}
);
```

require Block

A `require` block is used to load all the modules that are required to initialize the application, such as *ojModule* and *ojRouter*. Both are Oracle JET libraries required at this level to initialize the application routing logic.

The *appController* module is also imported at this point, which is an Oracle JET specific file that contains application wide logic and properties, such as the application name and routing configuration. We will be exploring more around the Oracle JET modules and the appController as we progress through this book.

Listing 2-2 shows what this `require` block will look like when you create an Oracle JET application for the first time.

Listing 2-2. Sample require Block

```
require(['ojs/ojcore', 'knockout', 'appController', 'ojs/ojknockout',
  'ojs/ojmodule', 'ojs/ojrouter', 'ojs/ojnavigationlist', 'ojs/ojbutton',
'ojs/ojtoolbar'],
  function (oj, ko, app) { // this callback gets executed when all required
  modules are loaded

    $(function() {

      function init() {
        oj.Router.sync().then(
          function () {
            app.loadModule();
            // Bind your ViewModel for the content of the whole page body.
            ko.applyBindings(app, document.getElementById('globalBody'));
          },
```

```
      function (error) {
        oj.Logger.error('Error in root start: ' + error.message);
      }
   );
  }

  // If running in a hybrid (e.g. Cordova) environment, we need to wait
  for the deviceready
  // event before executing any code that might interact with Cordova
  APIs or plugins.
  if ($(document.body).hasClass('oj-hybrid')) {
    document.addEventListener("deviceready", init);
  } else {
    init();
  }

});

}
);
```

Architecture Pattern

The MVC (Model-View-Controller) pattern is well known and has been used by frameworks for many years, especially if you come from an Oracle ADF (Application Development Framework) background. JET uses a different architecture pattern called MVVM (Model-View-ViewModel).

MVVM

MVVM is common in client-side implementations, due to its two-way data binding between the View and ViewModel, meaning that any data changes in the ViewModel are sent to the UI components, and any user inputs from the UI are updated in the ViewModel. The pattern helps to achieve a cleaner separation of UI code. Complex applications can quickly become tangled, and MVVM strives to prevent this by splitting the code into three areas. Figure 2-3 illustrates how the three areas are broken up within a JET application.

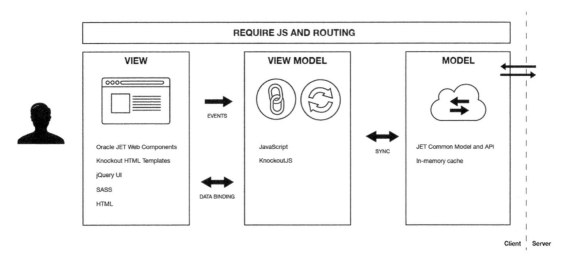

Figure 2-3. *MVVM architecture in JET*

Model

The Model is responsible for accessing the data stores using APIs, holding the data locally on the client and interacting with the APIs to keep the datastore up to date with any changes from the client. In JET, the model is handled by the *Oracle JET Common Model and Collection API.* These are a set of methods to handle the processing of data from the external API calls.

View

View is the most familiar segment of MVVM. It is the visual and interactive web page that end users will be seeing, and it showcases the data from the model to an end user through the current state of the ViewModel. In JET, it is the HTML and CSS markup of the page, powered by the JET Web Components and KnockoutJS declarative bindings.

ViewModel

The Model is responsible for holding the data, and the View is responsible for presenting the data. Think of the ViewModel as the intermediate. It exposes the Model data to assist in maintaining the state of the View. For JET, the ViewModel uses KnockoutJS at its core.

As a quick example, the structure of a ViewModel will be split into two areas. First is the ViewModel container, which is responsible for holding all of the data and application logic.

```
function MyNewViewModel(){
        // All ViewModel logic goes here
}
```

Next is an activation of Knockout. Use the following line of code to apply your new ViewModel to KnockoutJS:

```
ko.applyBindings(new MyNewViewModel());
```

Shortly, we will look into a real example of setting up a working ViewModel, using KnockoutJS.

Advantages of MVVM over MVC

Both MVC and MVVM offer a separation of concerns for an application. The problem with MVC is that the view can become large, as it contains both the View markup and the "code behind" logic that drives the functionality. The View is also tightly coupled to the business logic that sits behind it, meaning it is not really feasible to be able to easily swap out the View in the same way you can with MVVM.

The separation really helps when it comes to testing. With MVVM, you can isolate your ViewModel code and test it independently. Rerunnable, stand-alone unit tests become a lot easier to implement in MVVM.

Finally, MVVM enables design and development teams to work more seamlessly together on the same application. It is possible for design teams to work on the View layer HTML markup and CSS, without worrying about writing the business logic coding within the ViewModel.

KnockoutJS

Knockout provides the means to create rich user interfaces with JavaScript and HTML. These interfaces will feel more like a native desktop application, and this is because the code is actually running and processing on a user's machine (more specifically, a web browser) and not on a server, like traditional web applications. KnockoutJS will keep your View synchronized with your underline data model, using a combination of "observables" and "computables."

There are three fundamental concepts to Knockout: automatic dependency propagation, declarative bindings, and templating. Let's take a look at what each of these are.

Automatic Dependency Propagation

Using a combination of observables and computed values, KnockoutJS ensures that any changes to the underlying data model are automatically propagated to all dependencies, throughout the application. For example, if a user selects a postage method from a drop-down list at a checkout, the total value should automatically update, based upon their selection. KnockoutJS can be used to compute the new value and let any dependencies know of the updates, without the need to code any custom events and listeners.

In order to harness the dependency tracking, we must declare our variables and objects as observables, which is pretty straightforward to do. Take a normal JavaScript variable declaration.

```
this.myVar = 'Hello World!'
```

Wrap the value of the variable in the ko.observable function, to ensure that any changes are bubbled up to its dependencies.

```
this.myVar = ko.observable('Hello World!')
```

The variable this.myVar is now an observable, with all the resulting behavior that implies.

Declarative Bindings

Knockout uses an attribute introduced with HTML5 to create a binding between HTML elements on the View and the JavaScript objects within the ViewModel. This attribute is called data-bind, and there are many different bindings available, along with the ability to create custom bindings. An example of a binding is the text binding, which will display your parameter as text in the associated HTML element. Combined with the observable created earlier, the span below would output "Hello World."

```
<span data-bind="text: myVar"></span>
```

17

A few other notable bindings are

- *Visible*: This will change the visible state of an HTML element.

- *CSS*: This will change the CSS classes for an HTML element.

- *Attr*: This will change any attributes on an HTML, such as an ID. This can be useful when appending dynamic IDs to elements.

Using the previously mentioned scenario of a checkout, we will now look at combining observables, computables, and declarative bindings to produce a working example of postage calculation. You can view the code and have a go at modifying it yourself at the following JSFiddle workspace: `https://jsfiddle.net/practicaloraclejet/06hyrkfv/`.

View Code Example

Notice the bolded `data-bind` attributes in Listing 2-3. They are the attributes used to bind the HTML elements to KnockoutJS variables within the ViewModel that follows. The text binding is used for outputting a variable, while the value binding is used for inputting or changing a Knockout variable.

Listing 2-3. `data-bind` Attributes

```
<!-- Item information -->
<div>Item: Sugar Bowl: <span data-bind='text: purchasePrice'></span>
</div>

<!-- Postage Information -->
<div>Postage:
<select data-bind='value: postageCost'>
<option value='2'>Cheap postage</option>
<option value='5'>Super Deluxe Postage</option>
</select>
</div>

<!-- Total -->
<div>Total:  <span data-bind='text: totalValue'></span></div>
```

ViewModel Code Example

The ViewModel code in Listing 2-4 sets up the observables and computables to be used within the View.

Listing 2-4. Sample ViewModel Code

```
function AppViewModel() {
this.purchasePrice = ko.observable(13)
    this.postageCost = ko.observable(2);
    this.totalValue = ko.computed(function() {
        return parseFloat(this.purchasePrice()) + parseFloat(this.
        postageCost());
    }, this);
}

// Activates knockout.js
ko.applyBindings(new AppViewModel());
```

Templating

Often, in rich enterprise applications, you will have to use some sort of templating to build a view. A template in Knockout is essentially skeleton HTML, which can be used to build repeated chunks of code using data from your ViewModel.

A common example of where templates will become useful is within tables, wherein it may be required to have a certain markup or styling on a row and should be repeated for each row of data in the table.

It can also be useful when you have different elements on the page that have the same HTML markup but different data. That is exactly what the following example is demonstrating. Imagine that you are at a checkout, and you need to provide a billing address and a postal address. The data for these two could be different, but the template is the same.

View Example

In the View code shown in Listing 2-5, a single template has been created that is used for two different types of address (billing and shipping). The data is provided using the KnockoutJS data binding attribute data, and the template is assigned using the template attribute.

Listing 2-5. Code to Create a Single Template

```
<strong>Billing Address</strong>
<div data-bind="template: {name:'address-template',
data:billingAddress}"></div><br />

<strong>Shipping Address</strong>
<div data-bind="template: {name:'address-template',
data:shippingAddress}"></div>

<script id="address-template" type="text/html">
    <span data-bind="text: line1"></span><br />
    <span data-bind="text: line2"></span><br />
    <span data-bind="text: postcode"></span><br />
</script>
```

ViewModel Example

The ViewModel code in Listing 2-6 sets up the data to be used within the template defined previously.

Listing 2-6. Example of Code to Create a ViewModel

```
function AppViewModel() {
    this.billingAddress = ko.observable({line1: '42 Planet Earth', line2:
    'Orion Branch', postcode: 'N2 O2AR' });
    this.shippingAddress = ko.observable({line1: '1976 Mars', line2: 'Orion
    Branch', postcode: 'CO2 N2AR ' });
  }

ko.applyBindings(new AppViewModel());
```

The example in Listing 2-6 is available on JSFiddle from the following link: `https://jsfiddle.net/practicaloraclejet/njfr74xy/`.

Access the example from your browser. Then have a go at adding extra addresses or at modifying the template itself.

What Are Web Components?

Before we move on to looking at how we implement KnockoutJS within a JET application, first let's consider what Web Components are and why they are significant. Web Components are a collection of standards set out by W3C that package all the code for a specific widget into a custom HTML element. They do all this while being immune to any CSS or JavaScript already set on their page. This is achieved using the *Shadow DOM* (which isn't as scary as it sounds).

The Shadow DOM encapsulates a Web Component into its own private section of the page. Similar to how an iframe functions, but it isn't an iframe. It is essentially a nested DOM within the main DOM of the page. It is the Shadow DOM that gives Web Components their independence and prevents them being affected by other code within the page.

Using KnockoutJS Within JET

It is important to have a good understanding of KnockoutJS when using JET, as it will play a fundamental role in building your JET application. JET implements KnockoutJS slightly differently when binding to Knockout objects. The difference lies with the usage of the data-bind attribute, and although you can use the `data-bind` attribute as you normally would with a KnockoutJS application, it is encouraged to use the *Google Polymer* syntax instead. This syntax helps to provide an abstraction away from the binding technology. Google Polymer is an open source library for building Web Components, and the syntax is used to handle the binding between Web Components and KnockoutJS objects.

There are two different kinds of bindings to be aware of:

1. *One-way binding* `[[ ]]`: Using double square bracket binding indicates a one-way binding. A one-way binding will populate and update the View with the data stored within a ViewModel object, but it will not let the View update the object. Think of it as a read-only binding.

2. *Two-way binding* {{ }}: Using the double curly bracket (braces) binding indicates a two-way binding. A two-way binding works both ways: the View can update the dependent ViewModel object, and the ViewModel can update the View (in the same way it can with a one-way binding).

Taking our previous checkout implementation, we will now look at how we can implement the same functionality in JET. To view, modify, and use this code, head over to the JSFiddle and access the following URL: https://jsfiddle.net/ practicaloraclejet/Ljg8kt6e/.

View Code Example

Taking the existing View example, we have changed some of the elements to use a couple of Oracle JET Web Components and removed the requirement to use the data-bind syntax. Listing 2-7 shows the resulting code.

Listing 2-7. Using Oracle JET Web Components

```
<h1>Total value Example</h1>
<oj-label for="item-name">Item</oj-label>
<span id="item-name">Practical Oracle JET book - </span>
<span id="purchase-value" data-bind="text: '£' + purchasePrice()">
</span><br /><br/>

<oj-label for="basicSelect">Postage</oj-label>
<oj-select-one id="basicSelect" value="{{postageCost}}"
style="max-width:20em">
  <oj-option value="2.00">Cheap postage</oj-option>
  <oj-option value="5.00">Super deluxe postage</oj-option>
</oj-select-one>

<div>
  <br/ >
  <oj-label for="total-value">Total</oj-label>
  <oj-bind-text value="[[totalValue]]"></oj-bind-text>
</div>
```

Have a go at changing the two-way binding and removed the requirement to use the data-bind of the postageCost variable to a one-way binding, to see whether the calculation still works.

ViewModel Code Example

The ViewModel code is very similar to the previous example in Listing 2-7. Notice, however, that in Listing 2-8 we have combined the RequireJS code that we explored earlier with the KnockoutJS ViewModel code. In the require block, we are importing the libraries that this module needs to run, and this includes some Oracle JET components. The ojs/ojselectcombobox and ojs/ojlabel are two JET Web Components that we used previously within the View.

Listing 2-8. Combining RequireJS with KnockoutJS

```
require(['knockout',
  'ojs/ojcore',
  'jquery',
  'ojs/ojknockout',
  'ojs/ojselectcombobox',
  'ojs/ojlabel'
], function(ko, oj, $) {
  'use strict';

  var ViewModel = function() {
    var self = this;

    self.purchasePrice = ko.observable(25.00)
    self.postageCost = ko.observable(2.00);
    self.totalValue = ko.computed(function() {
      return parseFloat(self.purchasePrice()) + parseFloat(self.postageCost());
    });

  }
  ko.applyBindings(new ViewModel());
});
```

Oracle JET Webpack Support

Webpack is also a tool to load in libraries, and the newer versions of Oracle JET now include direct support for Webpack as an alternative to RequireJS. The way that Webpack loads libraries is different from RequireJS. It bundles all the libraries that the application requires into a single bundle when the application is built, rather than lazy loading them individually when required.

JET offers a Webpack plug-in, which can be installed by downloading it from the Oracle Technology Network (OTN): `https://www.oracle.com/technetwork/developer-tools/jet/downloads/index.html`. This file includes a README on how to switch an application over to use Webpack.

For the purposes of this book, we will be using RequireJS as the module loader, not Webpack.

BackboneJS (Common Model)

The Oracle JET Common Model is an implementation of the "active record" architecture pattern developed by Martin Fowler. The active record pattern wraps a single table row into an object, the object storing not only the data but also behavior permitted on that data.

The syntax of the common model is from Backbone JS, specifically *Backbone.Model* and *Backbone.Collection*. The best way to think of models and collections is this: a model is a single table row; it is a single object. A collection is the full table of rows (or models), as illustrated in Figure 2-4.

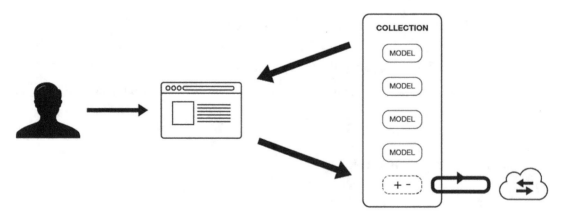

Figure 2-4. *Models and collections*

When creating a model or collection, you will have to use the `.extend` method to specify custom parameters (such as the URL of the API). In the following example, we are going to expand on an existing Oracle JET example from the Oracle JET "Getting Started" section and consume the end point (`https://apex.oracle.com/pls/apex/oraclejet/emp/`) into an *ojCollection*.

We will build upon the technologies explored within this chapter to build a table that includes the following:

- RequireJS, to import modules

- KnockoutJS, to create a ViewModel

- An Oracle JET table with KnockoutJS templating

- Implementation of the Oracle Common Model and Collection API

As we have not yet explored how to set up the structure of a JET application (I will cover this in Chapter 4), we will again be using a JSFiddle environment to build this example. The code is located at the following JSFiddle workspace: `https://jsfiddle.net/practicaloraclejet/pkbzwgu1/`.

The notable difference here is that we will not be implementing a `main.js` file. The RequireJS configuration will be included within the same block of code (similar to the previous postage example), and we will use the `require` function instead of `define`.

To begin, create a ViewModel and add in the RequireJS imports as shown in Listing 2-9.

Listing 2-9. Adding RequireJS

```
require(['knockout',
  'ojs/ojcore', // Imports all of the core Oracle JET libraries
  'jquery', // Imports JQuery
  'ojs/ojknockout', // Imports Knockout
  'ojs/ojtable', // Imports the Oracle JET table component
  'ojs/ojvalidation-datetime', // Imports a date validator
  'ojs/ojcollectiontabledatasource', // Imports the collection data source
  'ojs/ojvalidation-number' // Imports a number validator
], function(ko, oj, $) {
  'use strict';
```

```
    var ViewModel = function() {
        var self = this;
        // We will include our code logic here shortly
    };

  ko.applyBindings(new ViewModel());
});
```

Then include the RequireJS configuration, as shown in Listing 2-10. To reiterate, later in the book, this code will be within a main.js file, and we won't have to worry about the _getCDNPath function. The function is provided by Oracle's Getting Started example and is used to get the paths of the libraries.

Listing 2-10. *RequireJS Configuration*

```
function _getCDNPath(paths) {
    var cdnPath = "https://static.oracle.com/cdn/jet/";
    var ojPath = "v6.0.0/default/js/";
    var thirdpartyPath = "v6.0.0/3rdparty/";
    var keys = Object.keys(paths);
    var newPaths = {};
    function _isoj(key) {
        return (key.indexOf('oj') === 0 && key !== 'ojdnd');
    }
    keys.forEach(function(key) {
        newPaths[key] = cdnPath + (_isoj(key) ? ojPath : thirdpartyPath) +
        paths[key];
    });
    return newPaths;
}

requirejs.config({
    paths: _getCDNPath({
        'knockout': 'knockout/knockout-3.4.2',
        'jquery': 'jquery/jquery-3.3.1.min',
        'jqueryui-amd': 'jquery/jqueryui-amd-1.12.1.min',
        'promise': 'es6-promise/es6-promise.min',
        'ojs': 'min',
```

```
        'ojL10n': 'ojL10n',
        'ojtranslations': 'resources',
        'signals': 'js-signals/signals.min',
        'text': 'require/text',
        'hammerjs': 'hammer/hammer-2.0.8.min',
        'ojdnd': 'dnd-polyfill/dnd-polyfill-1.0.0.min',
        'touchr': 'touchr/touchr',
        'customElements': 'webcomponents/custom-elements.min'
    }),
  // Shim configurations for modules that do not expose AMD
  shim: {
    'jquery': {
      exports: ['jQuery', '$']
    }
  }
}
});
```

Now that the framework for this example is in place, let's build the application logic. The rest of the ViewModel code will have to be placed in the ViewModel function. Declare the variables that the example will use.

```
// API Endpoint
self.serviceURL = 'https://apex.oracle.com/pls/apex/oraclejet/emp/';

// Create observables for the collection and datasource
self.empCol = ko.observable();
self.dataSource = ko.observable();
```

Create the model and the collection and assign the collection to a data source.

```
// Create the Employee Model, using empno as the unique ID for model objects
    self.employee = oj.Model.extend({
        idAttribute: 'empno'
    });
    self.myEmp = new self.employee();
```

```
// Create the Employees Collection, assigning the URL to retrieve the
data from the API endpoint, and assigning the model created above
 self.empCollection = oj.Collection.extend({
     url: self.serviceURL,
     model: self.myEmp
});
self.empCol(new self.empCollection());

// Assign the newly created Collection to a datasource in a format that
the ojTable Component can understand
self.dataSource(new oj.CollectionTableDataSource(self.empCol()))
```

Finally, for the ViewModel, we must create a couple of converters for the date and salaries.

```
// Formatting data for salary fields
var salOptions = {style: 'currency', currency: 'USD'};
var salaryConverter = oj.Validation.converterFactory("number").
createConverter(salOptions);

// Formatting data for date fields
var dateOptions = {formatStyle: 'date', dateFormat: 'medium'};
var dateConverter = oj.Validation.converterFactory("datetime").
createConverter(dateOptions);

self.formatSal = function(data){
  return salaryConverter.format(data);
};

self.formatDate = function(data){
  return dateConverter.format(data);
};
```

The ViewModel is complete, so we will move onto the View, which will consist of an Oracle JET Web Component called *ojTable*. We will be specifying five attributes on this component:

id: Unique HTML element identifier

aria-label: Label for the component, used for accessibility

data: The data attribute is used to populate the component with data. We will be using Knockout to create a one-way binding between the observable dataSource and the ojTable component.

columns: Specifies the structure of each column. It is possible to set the headerText to be anything, but the field attribute must match the attribute names being returned from the service.

row-renderer: Specifies the template to provide to the component. The template will be repeated for each row in the table. Here we are telling the component to use the template of ID row_template.

Given the preceding components, following then is the View itself:

```
<h1>Employee List</h1>
<oj-table id='table' aria-label='Employees Table' data='[[dataSource]]'
columns='[
{"headerText": "Employee Number", "field": "empno"},
{"headerText": "Username", "field": "ename"},
 {"headerText": "Title", "field": "job"},
{"headerText": "Hire Date", "field": "hiredate"},
{"headerText": "Salary", "field": "sal"}
]'
row-renderer="[[oj.KnockoutTemplateUtils.getRenderer('row_template', true)]]">
</oj-table>
```

Creating the template is relatively simple, we use the <template> element and ensure that the id attribute matches the one that has been specified in the component, which is row_template. (See Listing 2-11.)

The template itself will consist only of HTML markup, and the data that is fed into the template is specified using data-bind attributes on the elements within the template. As we only want to output the service data to the table, we use the text binding, followed by the attribute (column) name from the JSON payload.

Notice the use of $parent. This is called a context property and is used for accessing data outside the table context. The formatDate and formatSal functions that were created earlier do not reside within the context of the data we are accessing for the table. Therefore, they must be accessed using the $parent context property.

Listing 2-11. Creating the Template

```
<template id="row_template">
    <tr>
        <td data-bind="text: empno">
        </td>
        <td data-bind="text: ename">
        </td>
        <td data-bind="text: job">
        </td>
        <td data-bind="text: $parent.formatDate(hiredate)">
        </td>
        <td data-bind="text: $parent.formatSal(sal)">
        </td>
    </tr>
</template>
```

The final output should look like the JSFiddle example shown in Figure 2-5.

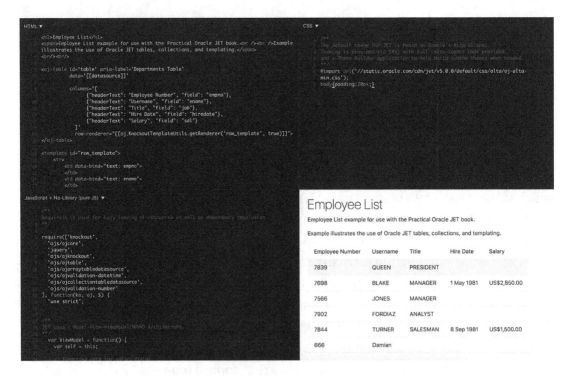

Figure 2-5. *Sample employee list*

Oracle JET Modules

In this chapter, you have seen how RequireJS and KnockoutJS can be used for modular development within Oracle JET. Code can be broken into separate `define` blocks and ViewModels. JET provides a component for encapsulating these separate code definitions, and that component is called an Oracle JET Module. Everything you will come to build within JET will be inside an Oracle JET Module (apart from the `index.html` file). We will be using ojModules for the different sections of the application, where they will be explored in more detail.

Summary

Throughout this chapter, you have learned the technical architecture of Oracle JET and how Model-View-ViewModel can segment the application structure and make it easier to develop cleaner UI code. You have also seen how KnockoutJS can be used to implement a MVVM application and how KnockoutJS provisions automatic UI updates and templating for more sophisticated tables and lists.

You have also discovered the drawbacks of including multiple JavaScript script tags, and how RequireJS can be used to asynchronously load in libraries and aid in modulating code.

Finally, you have seen how JET implements the BackboneJS syntax for Models and Collections and built a sample ojTable in JSFiddle.

Before moving on, it is highly recommended that you have a good understanding of KnockoutJS. Taking time to go through the interactive tutorial on the Knockout web site would be a great starting point.

CHAPTER 3

Support Ticket Application

In the first two chapters, we explored some issues with enterprise applications related to usability and how shortfalls in the usability of an application can ultimately decrease the productivity of end users. Oracle JET was outlined as a solution, and we have covered the basics of what makes up the Oracle JET toolkit.

Throughout the remainder of this book we will be building on the skills you have picked up from Chapter 2, to implement a functional application in JET. The application will be a support ticket system, which is often a system that people turn to when they are having difficulties with other systems or processes.

Support ticket systems for large companies can handle thousands of tickets a day, with many users and multiple levels of priorities, all at different stages in their support process. As users of a support ticket system are likely to be slightly more frustrated than average, it is important to get the user experience right. Waiting that few extra seconds for a support ticket to load, or difficulties finding tickets, could ultimately be the tipping point for losing business.

You will be building the application from the perspective of a user, and so that you are able to concentrate on Oracle JET, you will not have to worry about setting up a database or service layer. Instead, the book will provide mock data in the form of JSON payloads to get you started. You will, of course, be free to extend the application to include more functionality or write your own services to consume, if you desire.

This chapter will walk through the design for this system and includes low-fi mock-ups of how the system will look.

© Daniel Curtis 2019
D. Curtis, *Practical Oracle JET*, https://doi.org/10.1007/978-1-4842-4346-6_3

Scope

Before we delve into building the functionality of the system, we will first spend this chapter outlining the scope of the application. This will put you in a good position to begin setting up a JET application for the first time (in Chapter 4). Up until this point, you have been working with JSFiddle examples. Going forward you will be expected to scaffold your own JET application locally on your PC. Chapter-by-chapter versions of the code will be available on GitHub, if you get stuck.

The JSON data payloads for Chapter 3 will be made available on GitHub. Throughout the book, they will also be given at the start of the chapter in which they are used.

The APIs will be mocked using a tool called `mock-server`. Mocking end points can be really useful for front-end application development for a few reasons.

- We can quickly get the front end up and running, without the need to worry about setting up services and database environments.

- Front- and back-end developers can agree on the set structure of the end points up front, and the front-end developers can start building the UI straight away, instead of having to wait for the back-end developers to implement the service layer. This can greatly speed up the development process, and, provided the structure of the real end points matches the mock, they should be able to swap them over when the real ones are ready.

- Mocking is great for unit testing. It can sometimes be really difficult to replicate some scenarios with the real data set. Mocking the data means you have full control and can mock out all scenarios in your testing.

The functionality that you will have built by the end of this book can be broken down into the following:

- *Viewing list of tickets*: Viewing the list of outstanding tickets for a user

- *Searching for tickets*: Inline data searching to provide quick "as you type" searching, so users can get to their tickets faster

- *Viewing selected ticket*: Viewing a ticket and all of its replies chronologically

- *Replying to existing tickets*: A What You See Is What You Get (WYSIWYG) editor to reply to existing tickets

- *Creating new tickets*: Using a WYSIWYG editor to create new tickets

- *Closing Tickets*: Closing a ticket and specifying a reason why

- *Escalating ticket priority*: Escalating the priority of a ticket after the ticket has been created

- *Rating tickets*: Using one of the visualization components to rate tickets

- *Attachments*: To aid with support for ticket resolution, users can attach files to tickets using the ojFilePicker component.

Some of the Oracle JET Web Components that will be explored throughout the book are listed following:

- *ojListView*: `www.oracle.com/webfolder/technetwork/jet/jsdocs/oj.ojListView.html`

- *ojSwitcher*: `www.oracle.com/webfolder/technetwork/jet/jsdocs/oj.ojSwitcher.html`

- *ojAvatar*: `www.oracle.com/webfolder/technetwork/jet/jsdocs/oj.ojAvatar.html`

- *ojInputText*: `www.oracle.com/webfolder/technetwork/jet/jsdocs/oj.ojInputText.html`

- *ojTabBar*: `www.oracle.com/webfolder/technetwork/jet/jsdocs/oj.ojTabBar.html`

- *ojDialog*: `www.oracle.com/webfolder/technetwork/jet/jsdocs/oj.ojDialog.html`

- *ojMessages*: `www.oracle.com/webfolder/technetwork/jet/jsdocs/oj.ojMessages.html`

- *ojSelectOne*: `www.oracle.com/webfolder/technetwork/jet/jsdocs/oj.ojSelectOne.html`

- *ojRatingGauge*: `www.oracle.com/webfolder/technetwork/jet/jsdocs/oj.ojRatingGauge.html`

- *ojBindIf*: www.oracle.com/webfolder/technetwork/jet/jsdocs/
  oj.ojBindIf.html

- *ojBindText*: www.oracle.com/webfolder/technetwork/jet/jsdocs/
  oj.ojBindText.html

- *ojModule*: www.oracle.com/webfolder/technetwork/jet/jsdocs/
  ojModule.html

- *ojConveyorBelt*: www.oracle.com/webfolder/technetwork/jet/
  jsdocs/oj.ojConveyorBelt.html

- *ojButton*: www.oracle.com/webfolder/technetwork/jet/jsdocs/
  oj.ojButton.html

- *ojLabel*: www.oracle.com/webfolder/technetwork/jet/jsdocs/
  oj.ojLabel.html

- *ojFilePicker*: www.oracle.com/webfolder/technetwork/jet/jsdocs/
  oj.ojFilePicker.html

Some of the libraries that will be explored throughout the book are

- *Trumbowyg*: Used for the text areas as a WYSIWYG editor

- *Jasmine / Karma*: Used for unit testing the application

- *Signals*: Used to send signal events between different modules

Page Skeleton

The layout of the application will follow a standard three-column application layout. The left-hand column will be used for viewing and filtering open tickets, and the main content area will show the selected ticket and all its information. The box in the main section on the right will contain metadata about the selected ticket, such as information on the person assigned to the ticket, any ticket history, and rating information.

There will be a total of two menu bars. The main menu bar will hold the application logo, main menu navigation, and user information. The second menu bar will hold ticket-related actions, such as adding a new ticket and the tabs of the open tickets.

Note that the logged-in user text at the top right is in a more natural language format. This has been added to keep with the theme of improving the user experience. A simple change such as using natural language, can make the application feel a little friendlier, which, in turn, will make the user feel happier. Natural language additions such as this work great if an application is looking to adopt some sort of AI interface too, such as integrating the Oracle Digital Assistant Service into the UI.

We will be using a tab component for the main content area. This is so that users can have multiple tickets open at the same time. Having this kind of multitasking will be beneficial to bigger companies that have a lot of different support tickets open, or even for a support representative who will be dealing with multiple tickets and may have to keep several tickets open concurrently. The page skeleton is illustrated in Figure 3-1.

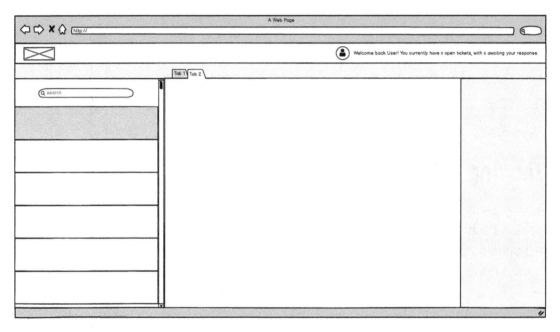

Figure 3-1. *Skeleton of application mock-up*

Ticket List

The leftmost pane of the application will contain a list of tickets, as shown in Figure 3-2. This list will be searchable using quick inline searching, which will give the user a "search as you type" experience. The search functionality will be built as a Web Component, giving it the full benefits of the Web Component architecture, which we will explore more later in the book.

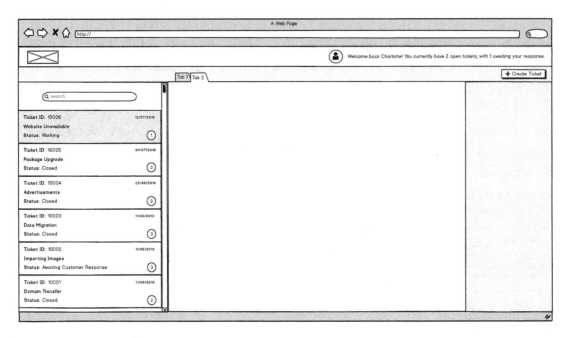

Figure 3-2. *Ticket list mock-up*

Viewing a Ticket

Selecting a ticket from the list will open the ticket in a new tab in the main content section. Each ticket will be assigned to a new tab, and the currently visible ticket will be highlighted in the list on the right-hand side.

The ticket view itself will show information about the current status of the ticket and options to escalate the priority of the ticket and close the ticket. Escalating the priority will move the ticket up one level, and users will be informed of this when they click the button. Before closing a ticket, users will be shown a pop-up asking them to confirm their action.

The first message displayed for a ticket will be the original support message raised by the customer; this will include the avatar of the user, the user's full name, attachment (if available), and their message. Following the original message will be all the replies by both support representatives and the user, all in the same format. Any notes from the user will be displayed on the left-hand side, whereas the support representatives' replies will be on the right. The amount of time since each note was posted is also shown.

To the right of the notes, users will be able to see information about their support representative, including a small bio and their average rating. The aim of this to reassure customers that they are in safe hands. Figure 3-3 shows selected ticket 10006 in focus.

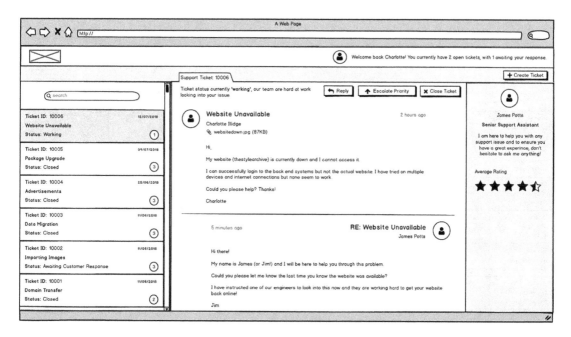

Figure 3-3. *View ticket mock-up*

Replying to Tickets

At the bottom of each open ticket (see Figure 3-4), there will be a box in which users can reply, using a WYSIWYG editor. The editor will be implemented using a third-party plug-in. The idea here is not to have a rich editor that permits images, HTML, etc., just a simple editor that can handle line spaces and some basic formatting.

Users will be able to upload an attachment with their comment, such as an image to aid with the support incident.

Clicking the Reply button at the top of a ticket will move the focus down to the reply box, so that it is easy for a user to get to the reply box on really long tickets.

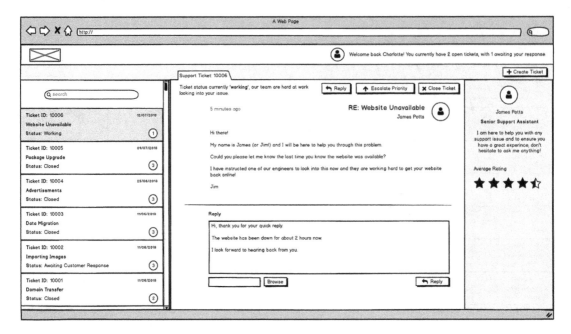

Figure 3-4. *Ticket replying mock-up*

Closing and Rating Tickets

Once users have received a satisfactory outcome to their support ticket, they will be able to self-close the ticket. To do this, they must click the Close Ticket button at the top of the screen, as shown in Figure 3-5.

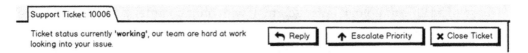

Figure 3-5. *Ticket buttons*

Clicking the Close Ticket button will show a dialog window asking users to confirm that they want to close the ticket. Figure 3-6 illustrates the ticket closure dialog, with a drop-down list to specify a closure reason.

Figure 3-6. *Close ticket confirmation mock-up*

Once they confirm, the ticket will then be closed, and the status of the ticket updated. The buttons at the top of the ticket will disappear and are switched instead to a rating component, with which users can rate their experience with the support assistant, as shown in Figure 3-7.

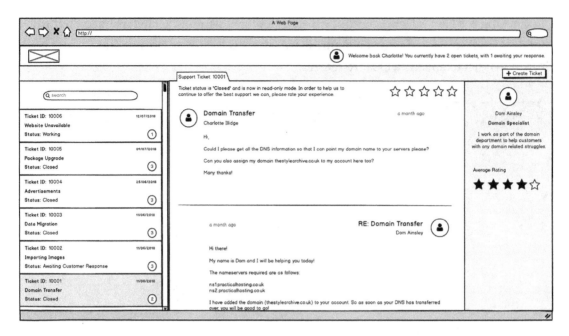

Figure 3-7. *Rating a closed ticket*

Creating a New Ticket

Clicking the Create Ticket button at the top right of the screen will cause the create ticket section to slide down. Here, the user will be able to fill out four fields to create a new ticket. The fields that will be shown are as follows:

- *Title*: The name of the ticket. Required field.

- *Priority*: Drop-down limited to values between 1 and 5, 1 being the highest priority. Required field.

- *Issue Summary*: A longer description to be used for detailing the issue. Required field.

- *Upload attachment*: Option to upload an attachment to the ticket when it is first created. Not Required.

Figure 3-8 illustrates how the create ticket section will look. The section will slide down and push the rest of the content farther down the page, making the ticket creation the primary focus to the user.

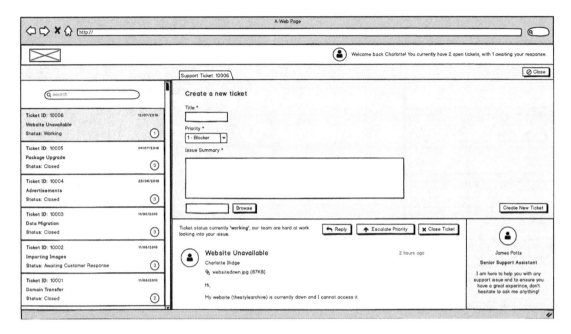

Figure 3-8. *Create a new ticket dialog mock-up*

Notifications

Notifications generated by the application will be shown in a box at the bottom right-hand corner of the screen. (See Figure 3-9). For example, if there is an error with the action a user is trying to perform, an error message will be shown. Success messages will also be displayed here, and the component we will use provides the means to easily set the type of notification.

Notifications will be global, and they can be dismissed by the user, by clicking the cross next to them.

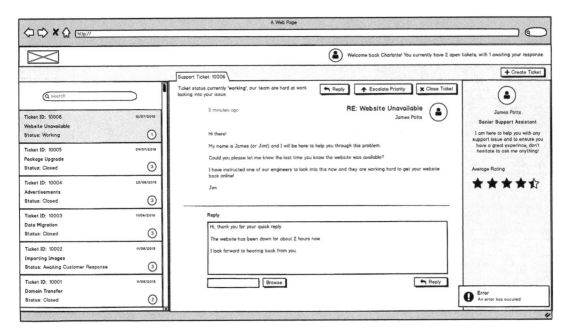

Figure 3-9. *Notifications mock-up*

Searching for Tickets

As briefly mentioned, users will have the ability to quickly search for tickets using a "search as you type" search box at the top of the ticket list. Search as you type gives users a better experience. It is similar to autocomplete on Google, in that it will start returning results to the user almost instantly, meaning their item may appear before they even finish typing a word. Combine that with not having a search button to press, and the time and effort for a user to find what they are looking for is greatly reduced.

Note in Figure 3-10 that the full search term has not been typed, yet the user can already see the item he or she is trying to search for.

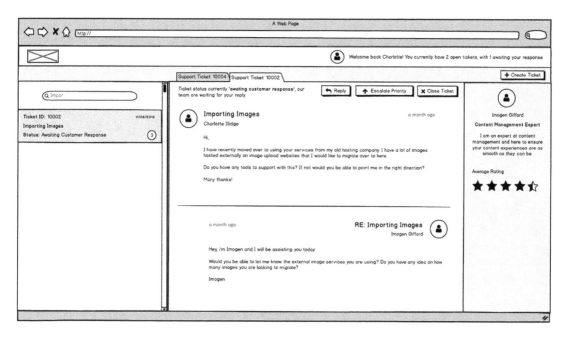

Figure 3-10. *Searching mock-up*

Summary

This chapter has provided an overview of the screens we will be building using the mock-ups provided, and it has also explored their functionality. Make sure that you have a good understanding of the expected functionality before moving on.

CHAPTER 4

Hello World

The JavaScript world can be a scary place and extremely overwhelming for newcomers. There are thousands of libraries, and with many doing similar, if not the same, things, it can be difficult to see the forest for the trees. The last thing you want to worry about is loads of build tools required to run the code you don't even know how to write yet! Luckily, Oracle JET makes the getting started process straightforward.

Throughout this chapter, we are going to look at how to set up a JET version 6 project for the first time and the prerequisites that are needed to set up a development environment. The Oracle JET web site (`oraclejet.org`) has a section specifically for getting started (Figure 4-1), so we will be using this as a guide, as we delve into more detail.

We will also look at how to install and manage the JavaScript libraries, using a tool called Node Package Manager (NPM).

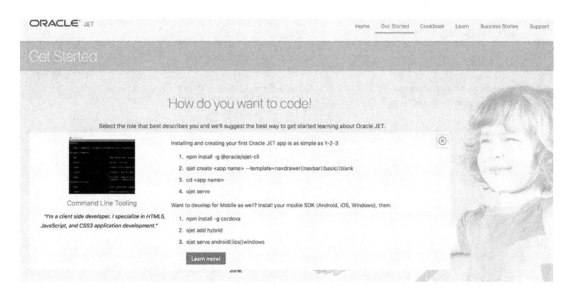

Figure 4-1. *Getting started with Oracle JET*

© Daniel Curtis 2019
D. Curtis, *Practical Oracle JET*, https://doi.org/10.1007/978-1-4842-4346-6_4

Environment Setup

The first task in setting up your first JET application is to ensure that you have *Node.js* installed on your machine. Node.js is an open source server environment, created for running JavaScript code on a server. It is simply an environment, built on Chrome's V8 JavaScript engine, which includes everything required to run a JavaScript program.

Node.js comes bundled with a package manager for handling JavaScript libraries (or packages), named Node Package Manager (NPM). NPM has a wide range of different JavaScript libraries within its repository. There should be a library on NPM for almost any scenario you encounter.

To install Node.js, go to `https://nodejs.org/` and install Node version 8.12.0. This version has support for Oracle JET Version 6, which is the version of JET that will be used throughout this book.

To find this version of Node.js on the relevant web site, click Other Downloads, then Previous Releases, which should bring you to the page `https://nodejs.org/en/download/releases/`, as shown in Figure 4-2. Navigate to Downloads and choose either the `.msi` or `.pkg` file, depending on your OS.

Figure 4-2.   Previous Node.js releases

Once Node.js has downloaded, verify the installation and version number, by running the following in a command window:

```
node -version
```

You can also check that NPM has been installed. Node.js will install the right version of NPM automatically:

```
npm --version
```

The primary command to be aware of with NPM will be the install command. To run the install command, simply follow the structure below:

```
npm install [insert library name]
```

The command `npm install` will look up the specified library on the NPM repository and install the library into a folder called `node_modules`. This folder will store all the JavaScript libraries installed via NPM, such as RequireJS and KnockoutJS. So, for example, running the command `npm install jquery` in an empty directory will download jQuery into an automatically created `node_modules` folder. (See Figure 4-3.)

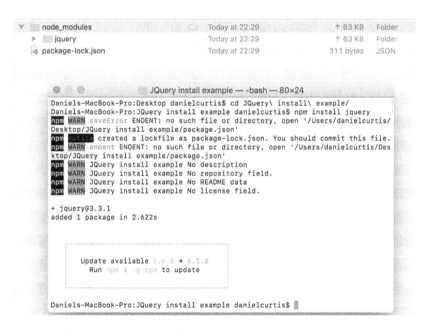

Figure 4-3. *Installing jQuery via NPM*

As well as having a node_modules folder local to the directory you are in, there is also a global node_modules folder stored on your machine. This should be stored under /usr/local/lib/node_modules on Mac, and %USERPROFILE%/AppData/Roaming/npm/node_modules on Windows. NPM is installed as a global node module when you install Node.js.

Oracle JET CLI

To develop an Oracle JET application, first install the Oracle JET Command Line Interface (CLI). The Oracle JET CLI is a command-line tool used for building and managing an Oracle JET application. Prior to the CLI tool, developers would have to run separate commands for *Yeoman,* to scaffold an application; *Grunt,* to manage build tasks; and *Cordova,* for mobile application development. These tools are now encapsulated into the one single tool.

As the CLI is a module that should be used globally across all JET projects, it must be installed using the global attribute by adding a -g into the install command, as follows:

```
npm install -g @oracle/ojet-cli@6.0.0
```

Run the install command, and you should have the ojet-cli module installed on your machine. You can verify that the CLI has been installed by visiting the global node_modules folder mentioned earlier.

Note that any modules that are installed globally will have to be installed individually by each person working on a project.

To find out more about the CLI tool, or if you require any help, you can run the ojet command with the 'help' attribute.

```
ojet --help
```

To check the version number of JET installed, use the 'version' attribute.

```
ojet --version
```

Integrated Development Environment (IDE)

The IDE that I recommend and will be using throughout the book for JET development is Visual Studio Code (VSC). VSC is lightweight, highly configurable, and has excellent GIT integration. It is possible to perform all your development, check out new branches, switch branches, commit, and push all changes directly within VSC. The interface is easy to use, and the way it tracks changes under the source control tab makes it straightforward to manage code changes.

Of course, any IDE can be used for JET development. You aren't tied down to using a single IDE, as you would be with other frameworks. If you prefer to use NetBeans or WebStorm, these can be used instead.

Another useful feature of VSC is the ability to have multiple integrated terminal windows open within the single window. All the commands needed for JET development can be run within the same application that you will be developing within.

To show the integrated terminal, navigate to View, then select Integrated Terminal, as shown in Figure 4-4.

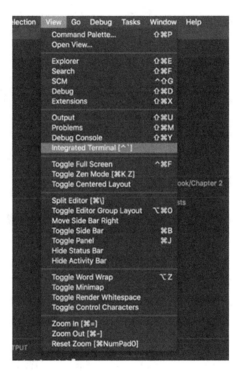

Figure 4-4. VSC Integrated Terminal

Scaffolding an Application

Scaffolding a JET application is essentially installing the base skeleton files of the application to get you started. The process is shown in Figure 4-5. First decide on your application location, navigate there within your terminal, and then run the following command:

```
ojet create MyOnlineSupport --template=navdrawer
```

```
Daniels-MacBook-Pro:~ danielcurtis$ cd Documents
Daniels-MacBook-Pro:Documents danielcurtis$ ojet create MyOnlineSupport —template=navdrawer
Processing template: navdrawer
Your app structure is generated. Continuing with library install.
Performing npm install may take a bit.
Invoking npm install.
npm WARN           coffee-script@1.12.7: CoffeeScript on NPM has moved to "coffeescript" (no hyphen)

> fsevents@1.2.4 install /Users/danielcurtis/Documents/MyOnlineSupport/node_modules/fsevents
> node install

[fsevents] Success: "/Users/danielcurtis/Documents/MyOnlineSupport/node_modules/fsevents/lib/binding/Release/
Pass —update-binary to reinstall or —build-from-source to recompile

> phantomjs-prebuilt@2.1.16 install /Users/danielcurtis/Documents/MyOnlineSupport/node_modules/phantomjs-prebu
> node install.js

PhantomJS not found on PATH
Download already available at /var/folders/k3/vz14xlms3tv7r_48xx7fy4vw0000gn/T/phantomjs/phantomjs-2.1.1-maco:
Verified checksum of previously downloaded file
Extracting zip contents
Removing /Users/danielcurtis/Documents/MyOnlineSupport/node_modules/phantomjs-prebuilt/lib/phantom
Copying extracted folder /var/folders/k3/vz14xlms3tv7r_48xx7fy4vw0000gn/T/phantomjs/phantomjs-2.1.1-macosx.zi|
—prebuilt/lib/phantom
Writing location.js file
Done. Phantomjs binary available at /Users/danielcurtis/Documents/MyOnlineSupport/node_modules/phantomjs-prebu
npm WARN qunit-reporter-junit@1.1.1 requires a peer of qunitjs@* but none is installed. You must install peer

added 653 packages and removed 1 package in 31.463s
Writing: oraclejetconfig.json
oraclejetconfig.json file exists. Checking config.
Your app is ready! Change to your new app directory 'MyOnlineSupport' and try 'ojet build' and 'ojet serve'.
```

Figure 4-5. *Scaffolding an Oracle JET application*

Running the create command will begin to scaffold an application with the
name "MyOnlineSupport" in the directory specified. It will then run an npm install
command, to install all the library dependencies.

Once the install has completed, create a new folder in the new MyOnlineSupport
directory called UI and move the entire contents of the MyOnlineSupport into this
new directory. So, all the new application files that you have just created are within
MyOnlineSupport/UI.

For the purposes of this book, we have created a new JET application with the
navdrawer template. There are four different template options available: navdrawer,
navbar, basic, and blank. The template determines what starting files and navigation
options are created when you initially scaffold an application. You can see a live
example of each of these types on the Oracle JET web site (www.oracle.com/webfolder/
technetwork/jet/globalExamples.html).

Application Structure

If you now open the project in VSC, by navigating to File ➤ Open and then selecting the project folder MyOnlineSupport, you will see the file structure of the new application in the explorer pane on the left-hand side, such as in Figure 4-6.

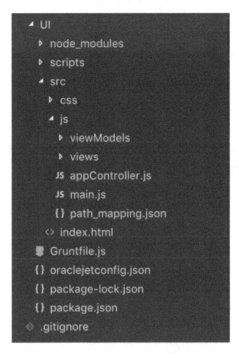

Figure 4-6. *Project file structure*

Next, we are going to take a look at the different files that have been created during the scaffolding process.

oraclejetconfig.json

The oraclejetconfig.json file is relatively small and includes some parameter configuration for paths within your application structure. For now, it is fine to leave everything in here as default. However, if you wanted to rename the folder location for the tests, for example, this is the place to do so.

package.json and package-lock.json

Both the package.json and package-lock.json files contain a list of dependencies that must be installed for the application to run. Whenever you run an npm install against a project, it will use these two files to work out what dependencies to install, and it will fetch the libraries and place them all within the local node_modules folder.

At this point, look in the node_modules folder. It will be full of hundreds of different directories that are dependencies for JET to run.

package vs. package-lock

You may have noticed that the package and package-lock files are very similar in nature. The truth is that they are indeed similar, but there is a history behind why that is.

When working within a project, if you come to install a new library, for example, trumbowyg (which we will be using later in the book), you can run the following command, and notice that trumbowyg will be added to the package.json file (seen in Figure 4-7), alongside the version installed:

```
npm install trumbowyg
```

```
{} package.json  ✕
 1    {
 2      "name": "MyOnlineSupport",
 3      "version": "1.0.0",
 4      "description": "An Oracle JavaScript Extension Toolkit(JET) web app",
 5      "dependencies": {
 6        "@oracle/oraclejet": "~6.0.0",
 7        "trumbowyg": "^2.11.1"
 8      },
 9      "devDependencies": {
10        "grunt": "^1.0.1",
11        "@oracle/grunt-oraclejet": "~6.0.0",
12        "load-grunt-config": "0.19.2",
13        "@oracle/oraclejet-tooling": "~6.0.0",
14        "qunit-reporter-junit": "^1.1.1",
15        "qunit": "^2.4.1"
16      },
17      "engines": {
18        "node": ">=0.10.0"
19      },
20      "private": true
21    }
```

Figure 4-7. `trumbowyg` *added to package.json file*

Note that the version of `trumbowyg` within the `package.json` file has a caret at the beginning (`^2.11.1`). This essentially instructs NPM to install the latest version of the major release line (so, the latest 2.x.x release). This means that if someone else were to check out this project in the future, and rerun an `npm install` following a newer release (such as version 2.12.1), they would get a newer (and, therefore mismatched) version to the one originally installed.

The `package-lock.json` file was introduced to overcome this inconsistency. The file contains a long list of the dependencies and the *specific* version that should be installed. It also includes extra information, such as the module location and a list of packages that it requires. If we take a look at my `package-lock.json` file after the install (Figure 4-8), we see that it also includes the `trumbowyg` installation and the exact version that was installed initially.

```
{} package-lock.json  ✕
4737        "integrity": "sha512-XrHUvV5HpdLmIj4uVMxHggLbFSZYIn7HEWsqePZcI50pco+MPqJ50wMGY794X7AOOhxOBAjbkqfAbEe/QMp2Lw==",
4738        "dev": true
4739      },
4740      "trumbowyg": {
4741        "version": "2.11.1",
4742        "resolved": "https://registry.npmjs.org/trumbowyg/-/trumbowyg-2.11.1.tgz",
4743        "integrity": "sha512-FtuxsO/6sP14HrjFArBK78CSQj6f8RYjv+oQ6vSygMwi5VknGOZAiml0nCwbgXyhICHVATvOquZA5sPFK21EdQ=="
4744      },
4745      "tunnel-agent": {
```

Figure 4-8. `trumbowyg` *added to* `package-lock.json` *file*

I can now be sure that if another developer joins the project, their working copy will be using the same versions as I do.

You should, however, always treat `package.json` as the source of truth. If you manually update the reference in `package.json` to a newer version of `trumbowyg` and rerun `npm install`, the newer version will be installed, not the older version, within the `package-lock.json` file.

Gruntfile

Prior to JET 4.0, Grunt was used as a task runner to build and serve Oracle JET applications. This is no longer the case, as the Oracle JET CLI has since replaced it. Grunt (and Yeoman, which was used for application scaffolding) will be removed completely in Oracle JET 7.0. Therefore, it is not recommended to use Grunt for registering build tasks. Instead, you should be using the hooks provided in the `scripts/hooks` directory.

scripts Directory
config

As part of the Oracle JET tooling, there are a lot of tasks that are run when either building or serving an application. For example, as part of the build task we will see shortly, JET tooling will copy over all the libraries required from `node_modules` into a staging directory. All of this is done by the core Oracle JET tooling library, and the files within the `scripts` directory provide the ability to extend the build tasks to perform custom functionality or commands as part of the build process.

In Chapter 8, we will be using the `copyCustomLibsToStaging` task to copy over a custom library that we will have to include and use within the application.

hooks

As well as using the existing build tasks, such as the `copyCustomLibsToStaging` mentioned previously, it is also possible to include your own build tasks. To do this, you must create a hook using one of the built-in hook points. The Oracle JET tooling defines various hook points and creates skeleton files for them when you create an application. These hook points are

- `before_build`: Triggered prior to the tooling kicking off the build process

- `before_release_build`: Triggered prior to the tooling kicking off before the uglify and RequireJS bundling occurs within release mode. (We will look at release mode shortly.)

- `before_hybrid_build`: Triggered before the `cordovaPrepare` build steps occur. Only applicable to mobile application development

- `before_serve`: Triggered before the web serve process connects

- `after_serve`: Triggered after the build process is complete and the application is served

If your company has a strict set of rules that must be passed before code can be committed to a shared repository, you will be able to use the `hooks` directory to run a linting process before an application is built. In this scenario, you would use the `before_ build` hook, located in `scripts/hooks/before_build.js`.

Source Directory (src)

The source directory is where all the pre-compiled application code will be stored. When creating a new project, JET will get you started by providing a basic template (in the form of an `index.html` file), some technology-specific configuration files (such as `main.js` and `appController.js`), and sample Views and ViewModels. Let's look at what each of these does.

index.html

The index file, as shown within Figure 4-9, will hold the initial HTML markup required to initialize the application. Some of this markup will persist through the lifetime of a session; however, most of it will be dynamically changed as a user interacts with the application. This is why most client-side applications are referred to as single-page applications (SPAs). The user remains on a single page (`index.html`), and the content of the page will be dynamically switched, compared to a traditional web site, wherein they would navigate between different pages (`about-us.html`, etc.).

```
ex.html ×
<html lang="en-us">
  <head>
    <title>Oracle JET Starter Template - Web Nav Bar</title>

    <meta charset="UTF-8">
    <meta name="viewport" content="viewport-fit=cover, width=device-width, initial-scale=1">
    <link rel="icon" href="css/images/favicon.ico" type="image/x-icon" />

    <!-- This is the main css file for the default Alta theme -->
    <!-- injector:theme -->
    <link rel="stylesheet" href="css/libs/oj/v5.0.0/alta/oj-alta-min.css" type="text/css"/>
    <!-- endinjector -->

    <!-- This contains icon fonts used by the starter template -->
    <link rel="stylesheet" href="css/demo-alta-site-min.css" type="text/css"/>

    <!-- This is where you would add any app specific styling -->
    <link rel="stylesheet" href="css/app.css" type="text/css"/>

  </head>
  <body class="oj-web-applayout-body">
    <!-- Template for rendering navigation items -->
    <script type="text/html" id="navTemplate">
      <li><a href="#">
```

Figure 4-9. *Index file of a new Oracle JET installation*

Much of the content switching will be performed within the ojModule located between the header and footer elements (shown in Figure 4-10). This is where the modulated views and view models will be injected.

```
      </oj-navigation-list>
    </div>
  </header>
  <oj-module role="main" class="oj-web-applayout-max-width oj-web-applayout-content" config="[[moduleConfig]]">
  </oj-module>
  <footer class="oj-web-applayout-footer" role="contentinfo">
    <div class="oj-web-applayout-footer-item oj-web-applayout-max-width">
```

Figure 4-10. *ojModule used for loading main application content*

In Chapter 2, we explored require.js and the main.js files. The require.js library and the main.js are both imported at the bottom of the index.html file.

The element with the ID of globalBody is where KnockoutJS will be bound to in the main.js file, after they are activated.

js/path_mapping.json

This is a relatively new addition to JET from version 5.0. It was essentially added to minimize the number of different places required to reference library files.

Prior to the path_mapping.json file, a reference to any third-party libraries would have to be added in the scripts/config/oraclejet-build.js file, then a reference in the main-release-paths.json file (which no longer exists), and finally a reference in the main.js file to set up the library to use with RequireJS.

JET 5.0 replaced main-release-paths.js with the path_mapping.json file, with the aim to reduce the number of places needed to include any library declarations. Using the trumbowyg library we have already installed, let's see how we can copy the library over into our application.

First open the js/path_mapping.json file, and add the following code anywhere in the libs object:

```
"trumbowyg": {
  "cdn": "3rdparty",
  "cwd": "node_modules/trumbowyg/dist",
  "debug": {
    "src": ["trumbowyg.min.js", "ui/icons.svg", "plugins/cleanpaste/**"],
    "path": "libs/trumbowyg/trumbowyg.min.js"
  },
  "release": {
    "src":  ["trumbowyg.min.js", "ui/icons.svg", "plugins/cleanpaste/**"],
    "path": "libs/trumbowyg/trumbowyg.min.js"
  }
},
```

What this will do is copy trumbowyg.min.js, seen in the screenshot from the node_modules/trumbowyg/dist folder (Figure 4-11), into the web/libs/trumbowyg folder that is created when you build or serve a JET application.

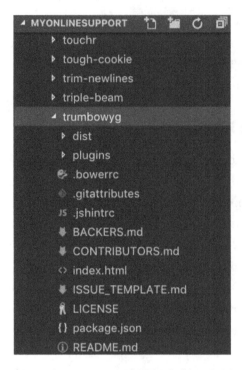

Figure 4-11. `trumbowyg` *file within the* `node_modules` *folder*

The separate debug and release objects provide the ability to have different parameters set for dev and release mode builds. This can be useful in copying over a minified version for production use. You will start to see this in action shortly, when we start to build and run the application.

JET uses a library called *Glob* (and *minimatch*) to match files and directories using patterns. Different patterns can be used to copy over whole directories or certain file types within directories.

If you would like to test out patterns, I recommend using http://www.globtester.com. It's a really useful tool for ensuring that patterns are correct.

js/main.js

The main.js file was explored in Chapter 2. It is the file which sets up all the JavaScript library configuration and initializes the application through the root require block. A main.js file is already included in the application, with all the JET library configurations in place.

As trumbowyg is installed and the reference to it included within the path_mapping. json file, we don't have to specify a path within the main.js file. Prior to 5.0, the following line would have to be added:

```
'trumbowyg': 'libs/trumbowyg/trumbowyg.min'
```

Now only the library identifier is required, and if it matches, JET will inject the path from the path_mapping.json file during build.

```
'trumbowyg': ''
```

js/appController.js

The appController file is responsible for setting up all the application-wide control logic, such as routing information and the logic for switching out the module responsible for the application's main view.

The ID of the router configuration must match that of the View/ViewModel name.

js/views and js/viewModels

All the Oracle JET module code should be placed within these two folders (views and viewModels). The naming and location of the files within these directories should be the same. So, for example, the dashboard.html in the views directory should have a corresponding dashboard.js file in the viewModels directory.

Oracle JET Build Tools

Now that we have explored all the files and folders that make up an Oracle JET application, let's take a look at how to build and serve an application. To do this, we will again be looking at the ojet command installed earlier with the Oracle JET CLI.

Building

To build an application, simply run the following command within the integrated terminal:

```
ojet build
```

The build command, as illustrated in Figure 4-12, is included among the Oracle JET CLI tools. It runs all the tasks needed to compile the project source code and required dependencies into a runnable application. After running the command, you will notice that there is a new web and themes directory in the file tree. Look in the web/js/libs/trumbowyg directory, and you should see the library we added earlier in the path_mapping.json file.

The web directory contains the compiled code. It is possible to take this folder outside of the project and deploy it anywhere. In Chapter 5, we will explore what the themes directory is and what it does.

Be careful here! It is easy, especially to begin with, to make edits to the files within the web (or themes) directory instead of within the src directory. If you do this and run build again, you will lose all your changes.

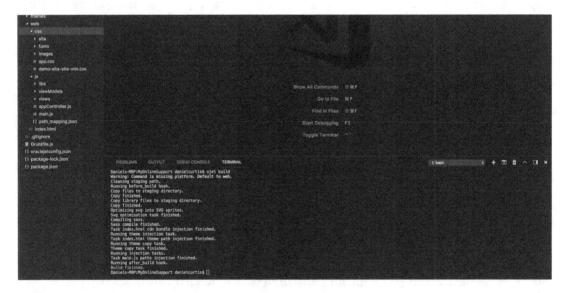

Figure 4-12. *Using the* build *command*

When the application is ready to be deployed to a production environment, you will want to build in release mode instead. Release mode will ensure that the code is optimized for production use, by minifying all the CSS and JavaScript code. To run in release mode, append --release to the end of the build command, as follows:

```
ojet build --release
```

Serving

Efficient and seamless development is possible with Oracle JET, thanks to the serve command. The process provides the ability to develop and see the result almost instantly.

Running the serve command "watches" certain folders within your project and recompiles the source code if a change occurs. The folders it watches by default are:

- All CSS files in src/css/ (including subdirectories)

- All JavaScript files in the src/js/ directory, except for the libs folder (including subdirectories)

- All JSON files in the src/js/ directory, except for the libs folder (including subdirectories)

- All CSS and JS files within the /src/tests directory

- All HTML files across all of the /src/ directory (including subdirectories)

It is possible to override the default watched directories by using the script/config/oraclejet-serve.js file to specify an array of files within the watch task. The files array uses the same global library mentioned within the path_mappings.json section for resolving path names.

The following example shows what would be required to watch files within a new directory created, called /src/js/toolkit:

```
watch: {
    sourceFiles:
      {
      files: [
 `${paths.src.common}/${paths.src.javascript}/toolkit/*.js`
],
}
        options: {
          livereload: true
          }
    }
}
```

For the purposes of this book, you will not be required to manually watch any directories. The defaults will suffice.

So, to serve the application, simply run the following command from a terminal window that has navigated to the UI directory:

```
ojet serve
```

What this will do now is build the source of your code and then launch a local web server on port 8000. It will then continuously watch for any changes in your application code and automatically open a browser window with the application loaded, as shown in Figure 4-13.

Figure 4-13. *Oracle JET application being served*

It is possible to change the default port from 8000 (if something else is using that port), by adding the `server-port` attribute when running the `serve` command.

```
ojet serve --server-port=8001
```

Now, if you navigate to `src/js/views/dashboard.html`, open the file and replace the text in the H1 element to be `Hello World`.When you save the file the watcher task will detect that the `dashboard.html` file has been edited, recompile it, and automatically reload the web browser window with the changes. This is demonstrated in Figure 4-14.

It is clear to see why this functionality is so useful. It can save hours previously wasted by having to manually rerun an application or deploy to servers to see the results.

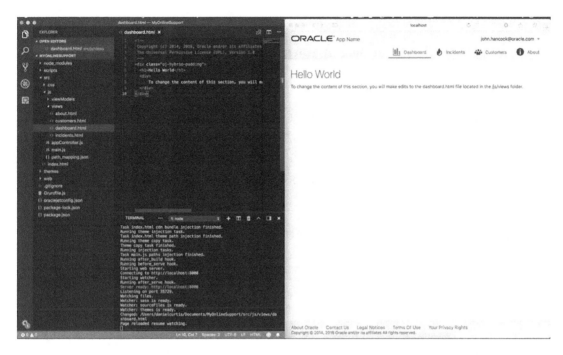

Figure 4-14. *Hello World*

Mock API Setup

To set up the API layer, we are going to use a plug-in called mock-server (www.npmjs. com/package/mockserver). If a chapter requires new mock APIs, the payloads will be included at the start of the chapter, and all the mock payloads will be available online in GitHub.

To begin, create a new directory, called API, at the root level of your application and another, called mocks, within the API directory. The structure should look like that shown in Figure 4-15.

Figure 4-15. *Folder structure*

Open a new terminal window within VSC, navigate to the API directory, and run the following command globally:

```
npm install mockserver -g
```

To set up the mock-server plug-in, you must create new files within the mocks directory that are named as REST methods. Within these files, you can include the JSON response payload and header information.

In Chapter 6, we will be building the ticket list view, and the API call to populate the ticket list will be a GET request to /tickets/. To return data on the end point, create a new file within API/mocks/tickets called GET.mock and populate it with the following data (Figure 4-16 shows what this should look like):

```
HTTP/1.1 200 OK
Content-Type: application/json; charset=utf-8
Access-Control-Allow-Origin: *

{
  "tickets": [
    {
      "id": 10006,
      "title": "Website Unavailable",
      "author": "Charlotte Illidge",
      "authorImage": "image.jpg",
      "representativeId": "1",
      "priority": 1,
      "service": "stylearchive",
      "dateCreated": "2018-07-12T16:20:47+00:00",
      "status": "Working",
      "message": "Hi, My website (thestylearchive) is currently down and I
      cannot access it. I can successfully log in to the back end systems
      but not the actual website.<br /><br />I have tried on multiple
      devices and internet connections but none seems to work. <br /><br />
      Could you please help?<br /><br /> Thanks!",
      "attachment":  [{
          "filePath": "images/websitedown.jpg",
          "fileSize": "87KB",
```

```
      "timestamp": "2018-07-12T16:20:47+00:00"
  }],
  "ticketRating": -1
},
{
  "id": 10005,
  "title": "Account Upgrade",
  "author": "Charlotte Illidge",
  "authorImage": "image.jpg",
  "representativeId": "2",
  "priority": 3,
  "service": "stylearchive",
  "dateCreated": "2018-07-09T08:37:17+00:00",
  "status": "Closed",
  "message": "Hi, <br /><br />I would like to upgrade my account to the
  next tier, so that I can include custom HTML in my templates, thanks!",
  "attachment": [],
  "ticketRating": 4
},
{
  "id": 10004,
  "title": "Advertisements",
  "author": "Charlotte Illidge",
  "authorImage": "image.jpg",
  "representativeId": "3",
  "priority": 3,
  "service": "stylearchive",
  "dateCreated": "2018-06-25T14:54:17+00:00",
  "status": "Closed",
  "message": "Hi, <br /><br />I would like to include AdSense
  advertisements on my website, but I cannot seem to find a way to do
  this. <br /><br />Is this possible? <br /><br />Thanks.",
  "attachment": [],
  "ticketRating": 5
},
```

```json
  {
    "id": 10003,
    "title": "Data Migration",
    "author": "Charlotte Illidge",
    "authorImage": "image.jpg",
    "representativeId": "4",
    "priority": 3,
    "service": "stylearchive",
    "dateCreated": "2018-06-11T11:22:16+00:00",
    "status": "Closed",
    "message": "Hi, I need to transfer all my data from my old provider
to you. <br /><br />I have a copy of the SQL dump. <br /><br />How do
I import this? <br /><br />Thanks,<br /> Charlotte.",
    "attachment": [],
    "ticketRating": 4
  },
  {
    "id": 10002,
    "title": "Importing Image",
    "author": "Charlotte Illidge",
    "authorImage": "image.jpg",
    "representativeId": "5",
    "priority": 3,
    "service": "stylearchive",
    "dateCreated": "2018-06-11T17:20:24+00:00",
    "status": "Awaiting Customer Response",
    "message": "Hi,<br /><br /> I have recently moved over to using your
services from my old hosting company. I have a lot of images hosted
externally on image upload websites that I would like to migrate over
to here.<br /><br />Do you have any tools to support with this? If
not would you be able to point me in the right direction?<br /><br />
Many thanks!",
    "attachment": [],
    "ticketRating": -1
```

```
  },
  {
    "id": 10001,
    "title": "Domain Transfer",
    "author": "Charlotte Illidge",
    "authorImage": "image.jpg",
    "representativeId": "6",
    "priority": 2,
    "service": "stylearchive",
    "dateCreated": "2018-06-11T17:22:29+00:00",
    "status": "Closed",
    "message": "Hi, Could I please get all the DNS information so that I
    can point my domain name to your servers please? <br /><br />Can you
    also assign my domain thestylearchive.co.uk to my account here too?
    <br /><br />Many thanks!",
    "attachment": [],
    "ticketRating": 5
  }
]
}
```

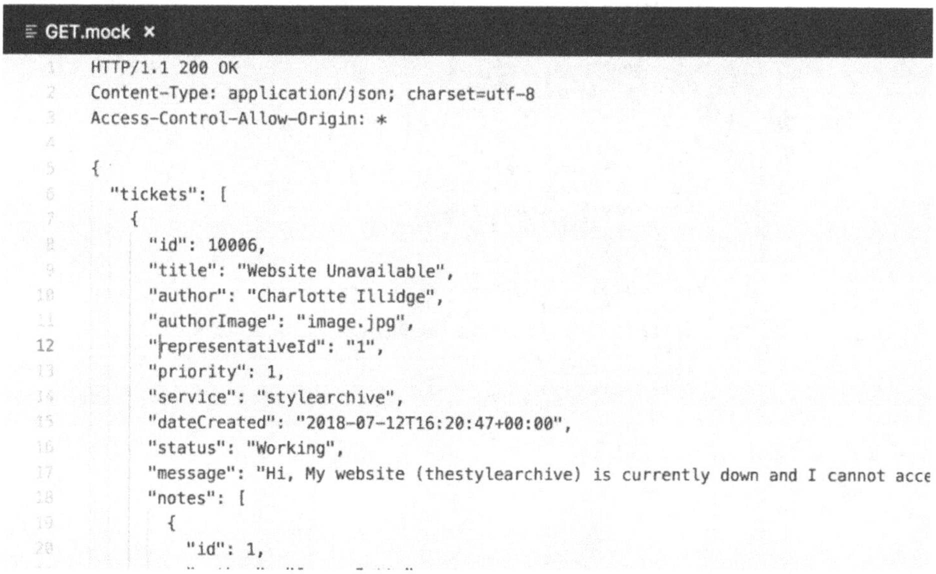

Figure 4-16. *Tickets GET response file*

Finally, you can start the mock server by running the following command:

```
mockserver -p 8080 -m  mocks
```

This initializes the mock server on port 8080, so if you visit `http://localhost:8080/tickets`, you should get a valid response with a formatted JSON payload, similar to that in Figure 4-17.

```
{
  "tickets": [
    {
      "id": 10006,
      "title": "Website Unavailable",
      "author": "Charlotte Illidge",
      "authorImage": "image.jpg",
      "representativeId": "1",
      "priority": 1,
      "service": "stylearchive",
      "dateCreated": "2018-07-12T16:20:47+00:00",
      "status": "Working",
      "message": "Hi, My website (thestylearchive) is curren
<br />I have tried on multiple devices and internet connecti
      "attachment":  [{
          "filePath": "images/websitedown.jpg",
          "fileSize": "87KB",
          "timestamp": "2018-07-12T16:20:47+00:00"
      }],
      "ticketRating": -1
    },
    {
      "id": 10005,
      "title": "Account Upgrade",
      "author": "Charlotte Illidge",
      "authorImage": "image.jpg",
      "representativeId": "2",
      "priority": 3,
      "service": "stylearchive",
      "dateCreated": "2018-07-09T08:37:17+00:00",
      "status": "Closed",
      "message": "Hi, <br /><br />I would like to upgrade my
      "attachment": [],
      "ticketRating": 4
    },
    {
      "id": 10004,
      "title": "Advertisements",
      "author": "Charlotte Illidge",
      "authorImage": "image.jpg",
      "representativeId": "3",
      "priority": 3,
      "service": "stylearchive",
      "dateCreated": "2018-06-25T14:54:17+00:00",
      "status": "Closed",
      "message": "Hi, <br /><br />I would like to include Ad
<br />Thanks.",
      "attachment": [],
      "ticketRating": 5
```

Figure 4-17. *Tickets response*

Summary

Following the completion of this chapter you will have a project ready to begin building an Oracle JET application, as well an understanding of the following:

1. How to install Node.js on a machine and what NPM is used for

2. How to install the Oracle JET CLI

3. How to create your first Oracle JET application, using the Oracle JET CLI

4. The file structure and scaffolded files in a new Oracle JET project

5. How to build and serve your first Oracle JET project

6. How to install and run a mock server

CHAPTER 5

Theming

A theme is a set of style rules that applies to the entire application. These rules are usually split into separate CSS files, alongside images and fonts, and contained within a single location known as the theme folder.

Application theming is extremely important, yet often overlooked. Despite theming getting more consideration, there is still a lot that can be improved. The struggles with theming in enterprise applications can be pinpointed to several factors, including the following:

- Where systems have transitioned from older paper-based systems, there may be a tendency for the system to replicate the design or theme of the paper forms that preceded, instead of rethinking for the digital implementation.

- The technology stack has made it difficult for implementing a theme. Prior to CSS3, most web sites were built using a combination of tables (instead of divs), and images were used to style the pages. This resulted in themes that were built of many "sliced" images that were difficult to modify and extend. Often, a small change to the layout would require a complete redesign of the page structure.

- Design and user experience were not as forefront as they are today. Functionality drove.

Why Is Theming Important?

A common reason for theming an application is to ensure that it follows your company branding guidelines, as it can help to provide consistency across applications, build brand recognition, and showcase a unique look to users. The theme of an application could be the difference between a customer staying or moving to a competitor.

© Daniel Curtis 2019
D. Curtis, *Practical Oracle JET*, https://doi.org/10.1007/978-1-4842-4346-6_5

If the application is an internal business application, ensuring that a suitable theme is in place can keep employees happier and in turn increase productivity. Users may be logging on to these applications day in, day out. A clunky looking application is going to make their experience (and, therefore, job) more miserable.

A theme is not just about the colors or font sizes. It is about the way that an element responds to user interaction, or the way that elements should be positioned on a page. Considering these aspects is critical to the user experience.

A theme is ultimately the face of a product. If the face is ugly, frustrating, or causes the user distress, the user will be put off the product, possibly until a new theme is used. Therefore, getting it right from the outset could be make or break.

Use of Default Theming

If possible, you should avoid using the default theme that comes with a product or framework. A default theme that has been used across multiple different applications can blur the lines for consumers. Imagine you have a really bad experience with a mobile banking application and decide to look elsewhere for your banking services. You look into another bank and find out that their mobile application uses the same software as the previous bank, just with a different logo or color scheme. Due to your experience with the previous bank's app, you will likely avoid this one too, for fear of the same issue. Therefore, you want a toolkit that provides the ability to easily extend or replace the default theme.

Oracle-Supplied Themes

There are two Oracle-supplied themes to be aware of. These are Skyros and Alta. Skyros was the old default, and Alta is a newer and more modern default.

Oracle Skyros Theme

Oracle ADF applications prior to 12c came with a default theme called Skyros. Figure 5-1 shows a sample theme. Those who have worked with ADF before will recognize the theme, and comparing with the standards of applications today, it may look a little dated.

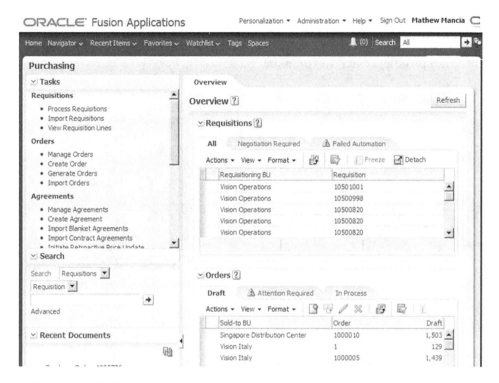

Figure 5-1. *Oracle Skyros theme*

One of the issues that come with theming ADF applications is the difficulty of changing elements of the theme. Trying to hook on to the classes for components in ADF can be difficult, and it is therefore easier to just use the default Skyros look and feel. This kind of scenario has resulted in a lot of applications that share the same theme, and at first glance, you might not be able to tell the difference between them. This is not limited to ADF either. Oracle forms applications were affected by this too, and many other non-Oracle applications end up with the default look and feel.

The Skyros theme and markup are quite heavy to load. It contains a lot of images and contributes to a slower performance on page load.

Oracle Alta Theme

Alongside the release of 12c, Oracle introduced a new theme named Alta UI. Figure 5-2 shows an example of this theme, which is cleaner, feels lighter, and is more responsive than its predecessor. It comes with extensive documentation of guidelines and best practices, including information such as behavior, usage, and appearance of elements, to help designers and developers get the most out of the theme. The Alta theme is deeply ingrained into the Oracle Cloud products, showcasing a common experience within the different cloud products currently on offer.

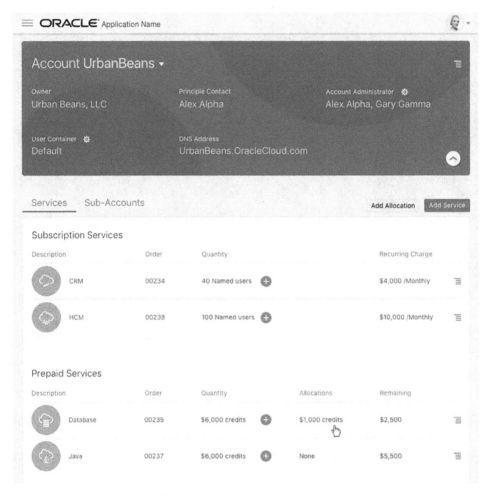

Figure 5-2. *Oracle Alta theme*

The Alta theme is available across all Fusion Middleware, Mobile Application Framework (MAF), and JET products, which can aid with consistency when a combination of products are used. It is designed to be responsive, with a separate set of patterns for mobile and web development.

Oracle Alta UI continues to evolve today and is really the centerpiece of theming in an Oracle JET application. The default theme is Alta, and unlike the pain and struggles in trying to modify or extend the Skyros theme in ADF, Alta in Oracle JET is designed to be modified and extended.

For our application, we are going to be using the Alta theme as our base and extending it out slightly to fit our designs.

SASS and CSS Custom Properties

CSS3 brought many great additions to the world of style sheets but still has many limitations, such as a lack of variables, nesting, and inheritance we come to know and love from programming. As style sheets have become more complicated, Syntactically Awesome Style Sheets (SASS) was developed as a solution to try and resolve some of the complexity and maintenance issues than can arise with large style sheets.

SASS is what is known as a CSS pre-processor (it transcribes down to CSS code as part of the build process). SASS brings variables, nesting, inheritance, and more to CSS.

At the time of writing this book, SASS is the pre-processor in Oracle JET, but starting with JET 6.0, an insight into the future of style sheets has been demonstrated with the introduction of support for CSS custom properties.

Most newer browser versions now support CSS custom properties, which are essentially variables without the need of a pre-processor. This is beneficial because using pre-processors has limitations, such as not being able to change variables dynamically. With CSS custom properties, you can hook onto the variables with JavaScript and dynamically change them at runtime.

The support for custom properties within JET comes accompanied with PreCSS, which will essentially allow for us to get the best of the SASS features alongside CSS custom properties. It will also ensure that older browsers and IE11 are supported where custom properties do not work.

Custom properties are just an experimental feature in JET, with the aim for them to replace SASS in the future. For now, though, we will be working with SASS until the full support of custom properties comes to JET in later versions.

Working in SASS

Let's initially look at some of the features that SASS offers and see a few examples of how they can be implemented. We will then move on to creating a new theme and using some of the SASS features discussed.

Variables and Importing Partials

SASS files are appended with the `.scss` extension. They are often referred to as *partials* and help to modularize CSS into smaller maintainable chunks. Partials can be imported into the main CSS file using the `@import` function.

An example of how importing and variables can be used within SASS is demonstrated following:

_vars.scss

```
// This is an example of a variable declaration, which can be stored
// within a separate SASS partial called vars.scss
$font-color: #2F4550;
```

myTheme.scss

```
// This is an example of an import and use of a variable within
// the main theme file: myTheme.scss
@import 'vars';

h1,h2,h3 {
    color: $font-color;
}
```

The approach just illustrated shows how you might define all your site's colors in a single partial, using SASS variables. Then you can load and refer to those colors from all your other partials files. Color changes can be made in the one file and will be applied to all classes that reference the variable.

Nesting

CSS lacks a nested hierarchy, which can be missed when trying to write clear and maintainable CSS structures. SASS introduces a concept of nesting, which can help to form better structured elements.

If all span elements within a header element were required to have the same font color (we can use the variable `$font-color` created in the prior section), nesting could be used to show a clear hierarchy of classes.

```
header {
    span {
        color: $font-color;
    }
}
```

When processed into raw CSS, the resulting rule will look similar to this:

```
header span {
    color: $font-color;
}
```

Although the preceding is a simple scenario, in larger applications, it is beneficial to have a clear visual nested hierarchy that matches the visual hierarchy of your HTML markup.

Extend

The extend feature in SASS provides inheritance for CSS selectors, which can be useful when reusing attributes within multiple CSS selectors. For example, if you have a button that can be in three different colors (gray, red, and green), but there are some attributes of the button that should remain consistent across all three colors, it is possible to extend the shared attributes, as in the method shown following:

```
// Shared attributes
%button-common {
  padding: 10px;
  font-family: Arial;
  font-size: 14px;
  color: #333;
}

// Colored buttons
.button-green {
 @extend %button-common;
 background-color:green;
}
```

```
.button-gray {
 @extend %button-common;
 background-color:gray;
}
.button-red {
 @extend %button-common;
 background-color:red;
}
```

We can therefore see in the example that there are common attributes in the button-common class. This class is extended using the @extend keyword within the three button color classes. The attributes from the common class will be included within the three color classes when the CSS is compiled. Using this kind of inheritance can cut code repetition.

Mixins

Mixins are reusable CSS declarations, with support for parameters. They are useful for grouping CSS declarations and, like extending, can help to avoid code repetition.

```
@mixin button($color) {
   padding: 10px;
   font-family: Arial;
   font-size: 14px;
   color: $color;
}

// Colored buttons
.button-green {
 @include button(green)
}
.button-gray {
   @include button(gray)
}
.button-red {
   @include button(red)
}
```

Using the button example again, we have created a mixin that accepts a `color` parameter. The mixin can be used in multiple classes, helping to cut down the need for code reuse.

Theme Builder

The Oracle JET theme builder is a JET application that can be used to familiarize yourself with the way different themes affect all the JET components and can be a good starting point for theme development. You can view a live version of the theme builder from the following web site: `www.oracle.com/webfolder/technetwork/jet/public_samples/JET-Theme-Builder/public_html/index.html`.

The live version of the theme builder offers an interactive application with six preloaded themes to switch between and instructions on how to get the theme builder set up locally on your machine.

It is possible to create a theme directly in your application without the theme builder. I tend to use the theme builder only as a reference point and instead do the creation and setup of theme directly in my application. To create the theme for this book, we will just do it directly within the application we have already scaffolded.

Creating a New Theme

Let's explore how we can extend the Alta UI theme, by creating a new theme directly within the application we created in Chapter 4. Make sure that you already have the MyOnlineSupport application open within your IDE.

To create a new theme, first we must add SASS to the project, by running the following command:

```
ojet add sass
```

Now create a theme by running the following command (note that `mosTheme` can be anything; it is the name that will be assigned to the theme when the process creates the theme skeleton):

```
ojet create theme mosTheme
```

This will have created a new theme named mosTheme in the src/themes directory, as shown in Figure 5-3.

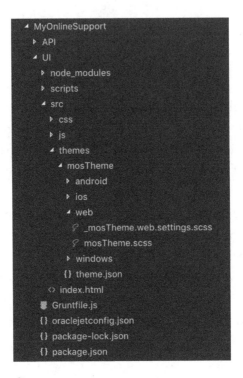

Figure 5-3. *New theme directory*

Note the four directories within the themes folder. These are three separate theme files for serving different variants of the theme on different platforms. We will be working in the web directory. This is the default platform when serving a JET application.

If you expand this directory, you will see two files:

1. _mosTheme.web.settings.scss: This settings file contains a long list of SASS variables that can be used for applying various styles across the whole of the theme. By default, all of these are commented out. Uncommenting a variable and changing its value will override the default value being set by the Alta theme.

2. mosTheme.scss: This SASS file encapsulates all the style sheets that will be combined to form the applications mosTheme.css file. This file contains all the SCSS imports required, such as the settings file, the Alta theme, and any other SASS partials developers include.

Including Custom SASS Partials

It is possible to override the default variables used by JET in the settings file, but inevitably, custom CSS classes will be required to style an element in a certain way. Custom classes should be contained within an SASS partial file.

To include SASS partials within a theme, first create a file called _vars.scss (SASS partials should be prefixed with an underscore) in src/themes/mosTheme/web/base and add the following variable into the file:

```
$font-color: #2F4550;
```

Next, create another file called _body.scss in src/themes/mosTheme/web/base and include the following:

```
h1,h2,h3 {
    color: $font-color;
}
```

Finally, include an import to the new file from within mosTheme.scss, by adding the following lines to the bottom of the file:

```
// Custom imports
@import "base/vars";
@import "base/body";
```

Now you must run the application with the new theme. To do this, you must append the theme attribute to end of the serve command and specify the theme name, as follows:

```
ojet serve --theme=mosTheme
```

Note   The same attribute can be applied when using the build command (ojet build --theme=mosTheme).

As the color change is subtle, you can confirm that the change has been successfully applied, by inspecting the element with the web console (using F12 on a browser will open the web console), as demonstrated in Figure 5-4.

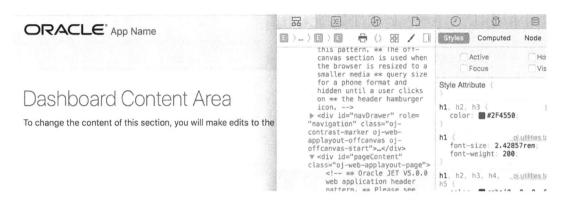

Figure 5-4. *Heading color changes*

The Three-Step Theme Process

The build process to themes is a little different from the rest of the application. Themes are staged before they are copied over to the web directory. When building or serving, any theme changes within src/themes are first processed by the SASS compiler and copied over the themes directory. This serves as an intermediate between the source and executable application code.

As you can see in Figure 5-5, there are three different theme directories, and this can be very confusing. You should never edit anything within the themes or web directory. Always make changes within src/themes, and let the build process copy the changes for you.

Figure 5-5. *The three-step theme process*

Summary

We have explored the theming processes within Oracle JET applications, by looking at the benefits that an open and expandable theme can provide and created our first JET theme. SASS is a fundamental part of creating clean and maintainable style sheets within an Oracle JET application, and we have looked at what SASS is and how it can be used. The theme created will be expanded as the application progresses.

CHAPTER 6

Creating the Page Skeleton

Now that everything is set up and the fundamentals have been covered, we can get to the good stuff by starting to build the application and seeing some real results! As the application is going to consist of a single page driven by Oracle JET modules, we will be setting up the structure of this single page by extending the existing template and themes we have already scaffolded in previous chapters.

We will also introduce several components, as well as CSS flexbox, which is used for structuring containers and elements of the page in a manner that is responsive. JET provides a collection of CSS classes out of the box to implement responsive layouts, and throughout this chapter, we will look at the most common ones and apply some of them to the application.

By the end of the chapter, you will have built the foundations of the application and used the following components:

- *ojInputText*
- *ojListView*
- *ojAvatar*
- *ojTabBar*
- *ojModel*
- *ojCollection*
- *ojBindText*

© Daniel Curtis 2019
D. Curtis, *Practical Oracle JET*, https://doi.org/10.1007/978-1-4842-4346-6_6

Flexbox

There was once a time when web development was a lot simpler, as the number of different devices and screen sizes were limited. With the introduction of smartphones in 2007, and the wave of different screen sizes that followed, a shift began toward the responsive web.

Initially, web sites started offering a "mobile" version of a web site that was often limited in functionality and was still not suited to several different sized devices. Making web sites responsive was more intrusive, as it often involved completely redesigning and rewriting a web site with different designs for different "breakpoints."

CSS3 introduced a new layout mode (an alternative to floats and positioning) called flexbox, which is an easy and responsive method of arranging elements on a page. To use flexbox, you simply have to specify the CSS attribute `display: flex` on the container elements, and any elements within the container (also called flex items) will automatically align into separate columns. Figure 6-1 illustrates the structure of a flexbox container with three flex items.

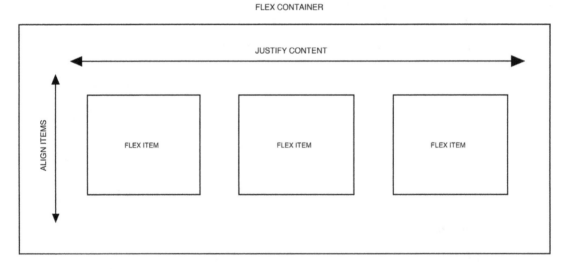

Figure 6-1. *Flex container with flex items*

The Flex Attribute

Once the flex container has been set up, the elements inside the container (the flex items) can have a flex property set against them. The flex property is a combination (or shorthand) of the `flex-grow`, `flex-shrink`, and `flex-basis` properties. These three properties are responsible for determining how much space flex items should be taking up within the container.

The three properties do the following:

- `flex-grow`: Number value that specifies how much the item will grow relative to the rest of the children within the container

- `flex-shrink`: Number value that specifies how much the item will shrink relative to the rest of the children within the container

- `flex-basis`: The length of the item; can be auto, inherit or a number followed by a length unit

The default values for the flex attribute are 0, 1, auto. This means that `flex-grow` is set to 0; `flex-shrink` is set to 1; and the basis is auto.

I recommend you look at this excellent web site: `http://the-echoplex.net/flexyboxes`. The site is a really useful tool when trying to work out how flex works and a great reference to come back to in the future when building new flex layouts.

Alongside the flex attribute, there are also several other attributes you can use with flexboxes. The following sections describe a few of these other attributes that will be useful and most commonly used within JET.

align-items

The `align-items` attribute aligns items vertically within a flexbox. This attribute has the following options:

- `center`: Positions the children in the center of the container

- `flex-start`: Positions the children at the beginning (top) of the container

- `flex-end`: Positions the children at the end (bottom) of the container

- `baseline`: Positions the children so that the baselines align

- `stretch` (*default*): The children stretch to fill the container.

justify-content

justify-content will position the flex items horizontally. If you struggle trying to remember the difference between align and justify, try to remember that justify positions flex items in the same way that the justify positioning works within Microsoft Word. The attribute has the following options:

- center: Positions the flex items in the center of the container
- flex-start *(default)*: Positions the flex items at the beginning (left) of the container
- flex-end: Positions the flex items at the end (right) of the container
- space-between: Spreads the flex items evenly across the width of the container
- space-around: Spreads the flex items evenly across the width of the container, but with space around the edges of the items

flex-direction

When setting a container to flex, the default direction is row, meaning the children will display side by side horizontally. Using the flex-direction attribute, you can change the default direction of the children to any of the following values:

- row *(default)*: Positions the children next to each other horizontally
- row-reverse: Positions the children next to each other horizontally, but in reverse order
- column: Positions the children under each other vertically, as a column
- column-reverse: Positions the children under each other vertically, as a column, but in reverse order

When changing the flex direction, you will also change the axis, and as a result, the align-items and justify-content attributes will inverse their default behavior.

flex-wrap

The flex-wrap attribute specifies whether the flex items remain in the same row, and overflow once there are too many, or whether they wrap onto the next line. The attribute has three values:

- nowrap *(default)*: Items will not wrap.

- wrap: Items will wrap, if needed, in relation to the direction set by the flex-direction attribute.

- wrap-reverse: Items will wrap, if needed, in reverse order.

Flex Within Oracle JET

It is not necessary to create CSS classes and use the flex attributes outlined earlier in this chapter when using JET, as the toolkit includes classes to help with implementing flex layouts. Having these classes available helps to cut down on the amount of custom CSS needed and declutters the SASS partials.

The toolkit classes also have responsive prefixes, to target different screen sizes. The responsive prefixes are as follows:

- *Small* (sm): Range of 0–767px

- *Medium* (md): Range of 768px–1023px

- *Large* (lg): Range of 1024px–1280px

- *Extra large* (xl): 1281px +

- *Print* (print): Layout for when a browser's print option is used

Media queries, which are a common web development technique introduced in CSS3 for responsive development, always target the minimal value and above. Similarly, any class ending in sm will cover all screen sizes. However, if you also apply classes using the md and lg sizes to an element, the media queries will kick in to override the sm settings when screens reach those larger sizes.

The most commonly used classes available from the offset in JET are:

- `oj-flex`: Sets the display attribute to `flex`, the `flex-wrap` property to `wrap`, and adds padding to the children

- `oj-[size]-[cols]`: Specifies the number of columns an element will occupy, which can be between 1 and 12. For example, using `oj-sm-2` and `oj-md-3` on an element would result in the element occupying two columns within the small range and switching to three columns in the medium range.

- `oj-[size]-justify-content-[value]`: Specifies the horizontal position of the container's children, using the same values outlined previously: `center`, `flex-start`, `flex-end`, `space-between`, and `space-around`

- `oj-[size]-align-items-[value]`: Specifies the vertical position of the container's children, using the same values outlined previously: `center`, `flex-start`, `flex-end`, `baseline`, and `stretch`

- `oj-[size]-flex-direction-column`: Switches the default direction from row to column

- `oj-[size]-padding-[multiplier]-[edge]`: Responsive margin and padding classes. For example, `oj-sm-padding-2x-end` would add a 2x padding to the end of the element.

I have covered some of the more common flex classes, and there are a lot more than can be used for more advanced layouts. A full guide to the available classes is available within the Oracle JET documentation and is useful as a reference. Here's a direct link to that documentation: `www.oracle.com/webfolder/technetwork/jet/jsdocs/FlexLayout.html`.

Setting Up the Application Structure

Time to dive into creating the structure of the page. Start by opening the application directory and rename the `dashboard` module files to `ticket-desk`. Make sure that you have renamed both the ViewModel file (`src/js/viewModels/dashboard.js`) and the View file (`src/js/views/dashboard.html`).

As the dashboard module name has changed, you must also update the router within the appController.js file. Open appController and change the reference to the dashboard within the router configuration to ticket-desk instead, so that it looks like the following:

```
self.router.configure({
    'ticket-desk': {label: 'Ticket Desk', isDefault: true},
    'incidents': {label: 'Incidents'},
    'customers': {label: 'Customers'},
    'about': {label: 'About'}
});
```

Ensure that your application is serving with the mosTheme. As a reminder on how to do this, run the following command from the application directory:

```
ojet serve --theme=mosTheme
```

Now we will be using flexbox to create the page containers. First, open the ticket-desk.html file and replace the contents with the following code. The markup will form the base container structure that will eventually contain all the application components and modules. It is split into three columns for the left and nine columns for the right. (There can be up to a maximum of 12 columns in an Oracle JET flexbox.)

```
<div class="oj-flex">
  <!-- Left Column Start-->
  <div class="oj-sm-3">
      Ticket List goes here
  </div>
  <!-- Left Column End-->

  <!-- Right Column Start-->
  <div class="oj-sm-9">
      Ticket Content goes here
  </div>

  <!-- Right Column End -->
</div>
```

If you apply a background color to the surrounding divs, you will notice that there is a padding surrounding the whole of your content. To have a full-width application, we need to remove this padding by opening src/index.html and removing the class attribute from the ojModule component that sits between the header and the footer. The ojModule should then look like the following:

```
<oj-module role="main" config="[[moduleConfig]]"></oj-module>
```

Including List Component in View

Let's move on to including the first component into the application. We are going to use the ojList component, which is an HTML list with advanced features, such as selection control.

Include the component within the left column.

```
<!-- Ticket List -->
<oj-list-view id='ticket-list'
      aria-label='ticket-list'
      class='oj-sm-12'
      data='[[ticketListDataSource]]'
      selection-mode='single'
      selection-required='true'
      item.renderer="[[oj.KnockoutTemplateUtils.getRenderer('ticket-list-
      template', true)]]">
</oj-list-view>
```

There are few attributes on this component to consider. We have assigned the class oj-sm-12 so that it spans the full width of its parent. The selection-mode attribute has been set to single, as we want one selection to be made at a time. There are two other options for the selection-mode attribute. These are 'multiple' (to allow multiple item selection) or 'none' (to disable selection altogether). We also want an item to always be selected, so the selection-required attribute is true.

The item.renderer attribute is used to specify the template to be used for each one of the list items. To create the template, include the following directly underneath the list view component:

```
<script type="text/html" id="ticket-list-template">
        <li data-bind="attr: {id: $data['id']}">
          <div class="oj-flex">
            <div class="oj-sm-8">
              <strong>Ticket ID:</strong>
      <oj-bind-text value="[[id]]"></oj-bind-text>
            </div>
            <div class="oj-sm-4">
              <oj-bind-text value="[[$parent.formatDate(dateCreated)]]">
              </oj-bind-text>
            </div>
          </div>
          <div class="oj-flex oj-sm-padding-2x-top oj-sm-padding-2x-bottom">
            <oj-bind-text value="[[title]]"></oj-bind-text>
          </div>
          <div class="oj-flex">
              <div class="oj-sm-8">
            <strong>Status:</strong>
                <oj-bind-text value="[[status]]"></oj-bind-text>
          </div>
              <div class="oj-sm-4">
            <oj-bind-text value="[[priority]]"></oj-bind-text>
      </div>
          </div>
        </li>
</script>
<!-- Ticket List -->
```

The template is applied to each row within the ticket list, and the values associated with each row can be accessed by their attribute key. As an example, title is an attribute that comes back from the API for each ticket and contains the ticket title.

For the date value, we are calling a function that formats the date and passing in the dateCreated attribute to the function. A formatted date will be returned once we set up the function within the next section.

Creating the List ViewModel

The ViewModel for the ticket desk must be set up to support the data being used by the Oracle JET list component within the View.

Open the file src/js/viewModels/ticket-desk.js and remove the contents that were created when the application was scaffolded. Once removed, the first section we want to add in is the define block. We must include some extra libraries within this define block, to load in the components we will be using within the module. These extra components are

- ojs/ojlistview: For loading the list component

- ojs/ojinputtext: For loading the inputText component we will be using later in the chapter

- ojs/ojcollectiontabledatasource: For loading the collection table data source, which is the object that encapsulates our data into a format accepted by the list view

- ojs/ojarraytabledatasource: Loads the array table data source module. It will be used for the tab bar implementation later in the chapter.

- ojs/ojmodel: For loading the model API, which will be used within the list collection

- ojs/ojvalidation-datetime: For loading the validation library that we will be using to convert the date into the right format for the UI

With the extra modules added, the define block and ViewModel function should look like the example below.

```
define(['ojs/ojcore',
        'knockout',
        'jquery',
        'ojs/ojlistview',
        'ojs/ojinputtext',
        'ojs/ojcollectiontabledatasource',
        'ojs/ojarraytabledatasource',
        'ojs/ojmodel',
```

```
        'ojs/ojvalidation-datetime'],
  function(oj, ko, $) {

    function TicketDeskViewModel() {
      var self = this;
    }

    return TicketDeskViewModel;
  }
);
```

Now we need to declare variables and set up the model and collection. Within the TicketDeskViewModel function, create ticketListDataSource as an observable, to ensure any changes to the data will automatically update its dependencies.

```
/* Variables */
self.ticketListDataSource = ko.observable();
```

Next, create a model object by extending the oj.Model function to pass in an idAttribute of 'id' when the model is declared. The idAttribute will be the unique identifier and reference for each model item.

When creating a collection, it is possible to specify several attributes. In this case, we want to specify the URL end point that will be used to retrieve the ticket list data. The model can also be assigned to the collection, using the 'model' attribute.

```
/* List View Collection and Model */
var ticketModelItem = oj.Model.extend({
    idAttribute: 'id'
});

var ticketListCollection = new oj.Collection(null, {
    url: "http://localhost:8080/tickets",
    model: ticketModelItem
});
```

Assign the collection to the ticketListDataSource observable, so that the component within the view is populated with the collection data. The CollectionTableDataSource formats the collection into a format suitable to be used with the ojListView component.

```
self.ticketListDataSource(new oj.CollectionTableDataSource(ticketListCollection));
```

Finally, create a small utility function for formatting the date within the list. This utility function uses the Oracle JET converter factory to format a date into a specified pattern.

```
/* Utils */
self.formatDate = function (date){
  var formatDate = oj.Validation.converterFactory(oj.
  ConverterFactory.CONVERTER_TYPE_DATETIME)
    .createConverter(
      {
        'pattern': 'dd/MM/yyyy'
      }
    );
  return formatDate.format(date)
}
```

Make sure that the mock server is running. As a reminder on how to run this, the command is as follows:

```
mockserver -m=mocks -p=8080
```

All being well, you should see a similar screen to that in Figure 6-2, which looks basic at the moment, but a lot is going on. We are retrieving data from an API and loading it into a working Oracle JET List View component that uses a template renderer. Through a very small amount of coding, we have achieved a good amount of functionality already!

Figure 6-2. *Ticket list*

Adding a Search Placeholder

Just above the list view component include the following code, which will be used later on to implement the search functionality:

```
<!-- Search functionality -->
<oj-input-text class="oj-sm-12 oj-sm-padding-3x-vertical oj-sm-padding-2x-horizontal"></oj-input-text>
<!-- Search functionality -->
```

Creating a Tab View

To help users multitask and have multiple tickets open at a time, we will use a component called ojTabBar. Tabs can be extremely useful on applications that have a lot of information on one screen, or where it is useful to have dynamic content displayed.

By using the example in the Oracle JET cookbook (www.oracle.com/webfolder/technetwork/jet/jetCookbook.html?component=tabbar&demo=tbaddremovetabs), include the following code into the second column of the ticket-desk.html file above 'Ticket Content goes here':

```
<!-- Tab Bar -->
    <div class="oj-flex oj-sm-padding-2x-top">
       <oj-tab-bar
        contextmenu="tabmenu"
        id="ticket-tab-bar"
        selection="{{selectedTabItem}}"
        edge="top"
        data="[[tabBarDataSource]]"
        item.renderer="[[oj.KnockoutTemplateUtils.getRenderer('tab-template',
        true)]]"
        on-oj-remove="[[onTabRemove]]"
        class="oj-sm-12 oj-sm-condense">
        <oj-menu slot="contextMenu" style="display:none" aria-label="Actions">
          <oj-option data-oj-command="oj-tabbar-remove">
            Removable
          </oj-option>
```

```
        </oj-menu>
    </oj-tab-bar>
</div>

    <script type="text/html" id="tab-template">
    <li class="oj-removable" data-bind="css:{'oj-disabled' :
    $data['disabled']=='true'}">
        <a href="#">
            <oj-bind-text value='[[name]]'></oj-bind-text>
        </a>
    </li>
    </script>
<!-- Tab Bar-->
```

The tab bar component accepts a number of different attributes, the most notable of which are:

- contextmenu: References the ojMenu component nested within the ojTabBar component, which provides a contextual menu for when a user right-clicks a tab. The context menu will have the option to remove a tab.

- selection: Binds to an observable that will hold the currently selected tab item

- edge: Specifies the location of the tab bar (start, end, top, or bottom)

- data: Binds to an observable that will hold the data to populate the tab bar component

- item.renderer: Like a list view, the tab bar can have a template for each tab item.

- on-oj-remove: Will call a function when a tab has been removed by the user

To include the variables and functions that sit behind the tab bar, open the ticket desk ViewModel and start by adding the following variables:

```
self.selectedTabItem = ko.observable("settings");
```

Next, include an array of sample data for the tab component (this will be replaced as we progress) and assign the data to the `tabBarDataSource` observable.

```
/* Tab Component */
 self.tabData = ko.observableArray([{
   name: 'Settings',
   id: 'settings'
 },
 {
   name: 'Tools',
   id: 'tools'
 },
 {
   name: 'Base',
   id: 'base'
 },
 {
   name: 'Environment',
   disabled: 'true',
   id: 'environment'
 },
 {
   name: 'Security',
   id: 'security'
 }]);
```

```
self.tabBarDataSource = new oj.ArrayTableDataSource(self.tabData,
{ idAttribute: 'id' });
```

Finally, we are going to include some functions for handling the deletion of tab items, provided by the cookbook example.

```
self.deleteTab = function (id) {
  var hnavlist = document.getElementById('ticket-tab-bar'),
    items = self.tabData();
  for (var i = 0; i < items.length; i++) {
    if (items[i].id === id) {
```

```
            self.tabData.splice(i, 1);
            oj.Context.getContext(hnavlist)
               .getBusyContext()
               .whenReady()
               .then(function () {
                  hnavlist.focus();
               });
            break;
         }
      }
   };

   self.onTabRemove = function (event) {
      self.deleteTab(event.detail.key);
      event.preventDefault();
      event.stopPropagation();
   };
```

Currently, the tab functionality is driven by the cookbook example, and the tab items, as shown in Figure 6-3, are just placeholders. We will be extending the tab functionality to our use case later in the book.

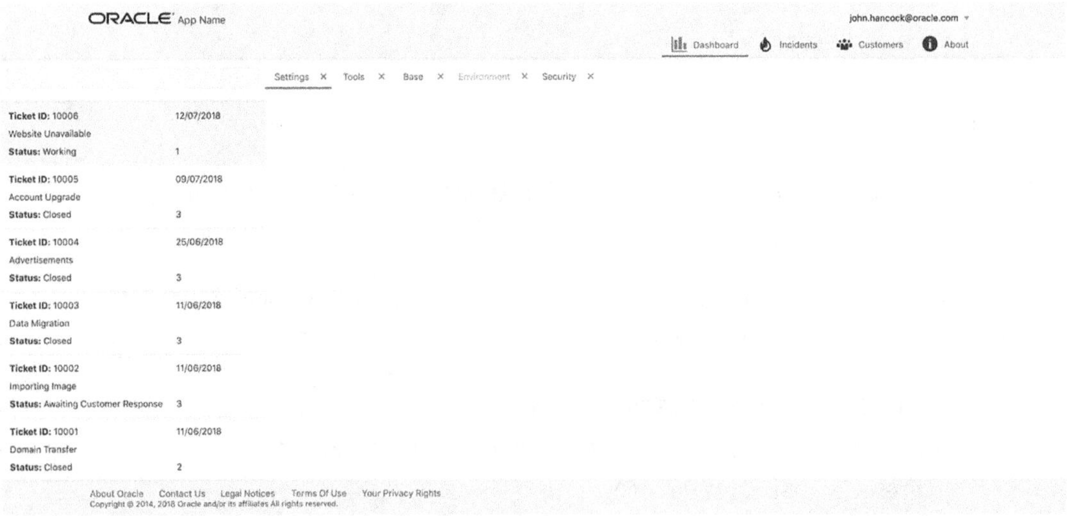

Figure 6-3. *Oracle JET tab bar*

Welcome Message and Avatar

At the top right of the screen we are going to add an avatar component, plus a welcome message with some information regarding a user's tickets. As we are developing the application within a single page, we will not require a top-level navigation at this stage, so we will be removing the menu bar.

To implement the avatar and welcome message, open `index.html` and replace the entire `oj-flex-bar-end` div and the navigation div that follows it with the following:

```
<div class="oj-flex-bar-end">
    <div class="oj-flex oj-md-align-items-center oj-sm-margin-2x-vertical">
        <oj-avatar role="img" aria-label="Single Placeholder Avatar"
        size="xxs">
            </oj-avatar>
            <span class="oj-flex oj-sm-padding-2x-start">
                Welcome back Charlotte, you currently have 2 open
                tickets, with 1 awaiting your response.
            </span>
    </div>
</div>
```

To load the avatar component, we must define it within the appController. Open the `appController.js` file and add the `ojs/ojavatar` module into the end of the `define` block. The header should now look similar to that in Figure 6-4.

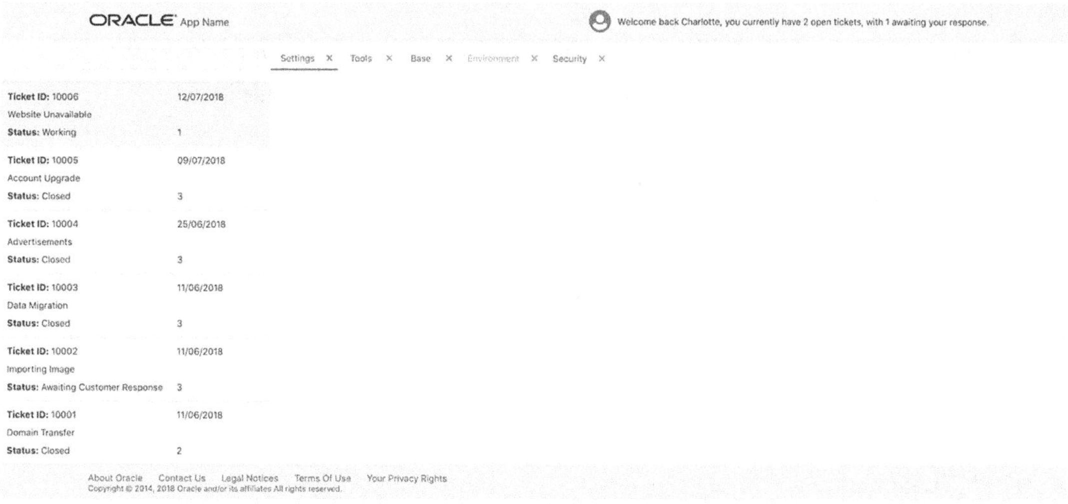

Figure 6-4. *Welcome message and Oracle JET avatar component*

Theming

Now that we have the functionality in place, we can make a couple of simple changes to make the application look more refined. The following sections describe several refinements that you'll find useful when creating your own JET applications.

Header Padding

Open `src/index.html` and on the header element, add the `oj-sm-padding-2x-vertical` class. Then remove the `oj-web-applayout-max-width` class from the first child div of the header element. This will increase the width of the header and add a small padding either side of it.

Removal of Oracle Logo

Still within the `index.html` file, remove the reference to the demo Oracle logo, which will be a span element with the class `demo-oracle-icon`. Then open `src/js/appController.js` and change the `appName` observable to `My Online Support`.

Setting List Container Height

To ensure that the height of the scrollable list view is correct, and that the height resizes for different screens, a dynamic height must be specified by using viewport height (vh). We can subtract the height of the header and footer areas to give us a dynamic height for the list view.

Create a SASS partial called `containers` within the base directory (`themes/mosTheme/web/base/_containers.scss`) and add the following class into it:

```
.list-view-container {
    height: calc(100vh - 175px);
}
```

Then import the SASS partial within your `mosTheme.scss`, so that it should now look like the following:

```
// Custom imports
@import "base/vars";
@import "base/body",
        "base/containers";
```

Finally, wrap the ticket list view in a new div with the classes `oj-flex` and `list-view-container`, and then you should be able to resize the height of the browser window and see the height of the list container adjust accordingly. The wrapping div should look like the following:

```
<div class="oj-flex list-view-container">
</div>
```

Adding Color

To give the application its own feel, we can define some colors as variables and then use them to color various areas of the system. To do this first declare some new color variables within the `vars.scss` file. Replace the existing contents of the `vars.scss` with the following:

```
$brand-color: #2C3E50;
$accent-color: #E74C3C;
$neutral-color: #ECF0F1;
$base-white-color: #ffffff;
```

If you are already serving the application, it may break when it tries to recompile. This is because the variable that we declared earlier in Chapter 5 (`$font-color`) will no longer exist and cause the compiler to fail when looking for it. Don't worry, open the body partial and replace the contents with the following:

```
h1,h2, h3 {
    color: $brand-color;
}

.oj-web-applayout-header {
    background-color: $brand-color;
    box-shadow: 0 8px 16px 0 rgba($brand-color, 0.2);
}

.oj-web-applayout-header-title {
    color: $base-white-color;
}
```

105

```
.oj-web-applayout-footer {
    min-height:0;
}

header {
    span {
        color: $base-white-color;
    }

    .oj-hover {
        background-color:transparent !important;
    }
}
```

Finally, open _mosTheme.web.settings.scss, find $brandColor, and uncomment the variable. Replace the hex code with the following:

```
$brandColor:            #788585 !default;
```

You may now have to serve the application again if it stopped earlier in this section.

Further Container Classes

To add further color and some shadowing to the containers, include the following classes within the containers partial:

```
.left-column-container {
    box-shadow: 0 8px 12px 0 $neutral-color;
}

.tabbar-container {
    background-color:$neutral-color;
}
```

Then apply the `left-column-container` class to the div that surrounds the entire left column, and the `tabbar-container` class to the div that surrounds the tab bar. Be careful not to apply the `tabbar-container` to the whole right-hand container.

Component Styling

Oracle JET components come with CSS classes already applied to them. When inspecting the ojTabBar, you will notice that each of the items within the tab bar have a class of `oj-tabbar-item`, as shown in Figure 6-5.

```
▼ <oj-tab-bar contextmenu="tabmenu" id="hnavlist"
selection="{{selectedItem}}" current-item="{{currentItem}}"
edge="top" data="[[dataSource]]" item.renderer="
[[oj.KnockoutTemplateUtils.getRenderer('tab_template',
true)]]" on-oj-remove="[[onRemove]]" class="oj-sm-12 oj-sm-
condense oj-tabbar oj-tabbar-expanded oj-tabbar-horizontal
oj-navigationlist-page-level oj-component-initnode oj-
complete" tabindex="0" aria-multiselectable="false" role=
"tablist">
    ▶ <oj-menu slot="contextMenu" style="display:none" aria-
    label="Actions" id="ui-id-12" class="oj-menu oj-component
    oj-menu-text-only oj-component-initnode oj-complete"
    role="menu" tabindex="0">…</oj-menu>
    ▼ <div class="oj-tabbar-listview-container" role=
    "presentation">
        ▼ <div class="oj-tabbar-listview oj-component" role=
        "presentation" style="max-width: none;">
            ▶ <div class="oj-helper-detect-contraction">…</div>
            ▶ <div class="oj-helper-detect-expansion">…</div>
            ▼ <ul id="ui-id-14" class="oj-tabbar-element" role=
            "presentation">
                ▶ <li class="oj-removable oj-tabbar-item-element
                oj-tabbar-item oj-selected" data-bind="css:{'oj-
                disabled' : $data['disabled']=='true'}" id="ui-id-
                16" role="presentation">…</li>
                <li role="separator" class="oj-tabbar-
                divider"></li>
                ▶ <li class="oj-removable oj-tabbar-item-element
                oj-tabbar-item oj-default" data-bind="css:{'oj-
                disabled' : $data['disabled']=='true'}" id="ui-id-
                19" role="presentation">…</li> = $0
                <li role="separator" class="oj-tabbar-
                divider"></li>
```

Figure 6-5.   Tab bar items

We can target these classes when necessary and add custom styling onto the Oracle JET components. Create a new directory within mosTheme/web called `components`. This new directory will be used to create partials that are needed for any component-specific styling.

First, create a partial for the tab bar component, called _tabs.scss, and use the following class, which will add a padding to the tab so that the text looks more central within the tab bar:

```
.oj-tabbar-item {
    padding-bottom: 10px;
}
```

Create another partial in the components folder named _list-view.scss and add the following:

```
.oj-listview-element {
    .oj-selected {
        border-left: 6px solid $accent-color;
    }
}
```

Make sure that you import the two new partials in the mosTheme.scss file. When you view the application, you should be able to see a red left border when selecting an item in the list view.

Footer

Within the index.html file, replace the footer element with the following:

```
<footer class="oj-web-applayout-footer" role="contentinfo">
        <div class="oj-web-applayout-footer-item oj-text-secondary-color
        oj-text-sm">
          Copyright &copy; Practical Oracle JET. Developed on Earth C-137
        </div>
</footer>
```

You may also remove the footerLinks references from the appController.js file, as these are no longer needed.

Summary

By following all the steps outlined within this chapter you should have an Oracle JET application that looks similar to Figure 6-6. You should have an understanding of how CSS flex works and how it can be implemented quickly and easily, using the out-of-the-box classes that JET provides. You will also have built your first JET layout in flex and included several components, as well as hooking up the list component to the JET Common Model and retrieving data from a mock server.

Figure 6-6. *Completed Chapter 6 outcome*

CHAPTER 7

Viewing Tickets

Time to get to the main act of the development. We will begin to create the ticket viewing and switching functionality, using a variety of components. By the end of this chapter, you will have an application that is essentially in read-only mode—perfect for showing your friends or coworkers this cool new JET application that you have put together but not for letting them click any of the buttons, because they won't work yet.

For this chapter, the following elements and classes will be used:

- *ojModule*
- *ojConveyorBelt*
- *ojListView*
- *ojButton*
- *ojAvatar*
- *ojGauge*
- *ojTabs*
- *ojContext*
- *ojArrayDataProvider*

As well as the components in the preceding list, we will also work more with computables, utility files, and the Oracle JET Busy Context.

API Setup

For this chapter, we will create new mock API end points. Create the files in Listings 7-1 through 7-12. Remember that you don't need to type the files in by hand. They are available from this book's GitHub page.

© Daniel Curtis 2019
D. Curtis, *Practical Oracle JET*, https://doi.org/10.1007/978-1-4842-4346-6_7

Listings 7-1 to 7-6 include the reply payloads for each of the tickets. Add these in the same way you have added the mock files previously and follow the directory structure outlined for each listing.

Listing 7-1. API/mocks/tickets/replies/10001/GET.mock

```
HTTP/1.1 200 OK
Content-Type: application/json; charset=utf-8
Access-Control-Allow-Origin: *

{
    "notes": [
     {
         "id": 1,
         "author": "Dom Ainsley",
         "timestamp": "2018-06-11T17:24:32+00:00",
         "note": "Hi there! My name is Dom and I will helping you
         today!<br /><br />The nameservers that you require are as
         follows:<br /><br />ns1.practicalhosting.co.uk<br />ns2.
         practicalhosting.co.uk.<br /><br />I have added the domain
         (thestylearchive.co.uk) to your account, so as soon as your DNS
         has transfered and propagated, you will be good to go!<br /><br />
         Any further questions - please let me know.<br /><br />Dom",
"attachment": []
        },
        {
         "id": 2,
         "author": "Charlotte Illidge",
         "timestamp": "2018-06-11T17:39:46+00:00",
         "note": "Hi Dom, thanks for your help. Everything seems to be
         working now.<br /><br /> Charlotte",
"attachment": []
        }
     ]
}
```

Listing 7-2. API/mocks/tickets/replies/10002/GET.mock

```
HTTP/1.1 200 OK
Content-Type: application/json; charset=utf-8
Access-Control-Allow-Origin: *

{
    "notes": [
        {
          "id": 1,
          "author": "Imogen Gifford",
          "timestamp": "2018-06-11T18:24:29+00:00",
          "note": "Hey! I'm Imogen and I will be assisting you today.<br />
          <br /> Would you be able to let me know the external image
          services you are using? Do you have any idea of how many images
          you are looking to migrate? <br /><br />Imogen",
"attachment": []
        }
      ]
}
```

Listing 7-3. API/mocks/tickets/replies/10003/GET.mock

```
HTTP/1.1 200 OK
Content-Type: application/json; charset=utf-8
Access-Control-Allow-Origin: *

{
    "notes": [
        {
          "id": 1,
          "author": "Reece Jacques",
          "timestamp": "2018-06-11T13:43:54+00:00",
          "note": "Hi Charlotte, <br /><br />We cannot upload that data for
          you, but it is really easy for you to do it! <br /><br />Head to
          your control panel, then to databases and hit the data import
          tool. Follow the steps and the data will be there in no time!<br />
```

```
        <br />Please let me know if you have any further questions.<br />
        <br />Reece",
"attachment": []
      }
    ]
}
```

Listing 7-4. *API/mocks/tickets/replies/10004/GET.mock*

```
HTTP/1.1 200 OK
Content-Type: application/json; charset=utf-8
Access-Control-Allow-Origin: *

{
    "notes": [
      {
          "id": 1,
          "author": "Oliver Butler",
          "timestamp": "2018-06-25T15:20:24+00:00",
          "note": "Hi Charlotte, <br /><br />You are not able to add the
          code into your website using custom HTML with your package. <br />
          <br /> Unfortunately in order to do this you will need to
          upgrade your package. You can find more information over on our
          services page. <br /><br />Please let me know if you have anymore
          questions.<br /><br />Kind Regards<br />Oliver",
"attachment": []
      }
    ]
}
```

Listing 7-5. *API/mocks/tickets/replies/10005/GET.mock*

```
HTTP/1.1 200 OK
Content-Type: application/json; charset=utf-8
Access-Control-Allow-Origin: *

{
    "notes": [
```

114

```
    {
        "id": 1,
        "author": "Nick Dobson",
        "timestamp": "2018-07-09T09:33:11+00:00",
        "note": "Hi Charlotte, thank you for your inquiry! <br /><br />
        I have now upgraded your account for you. <br /><br />You will
        now have received an e-mail with your updated billing amount and
        schedule. <br /><br />Please let me know if you have any questions.",
"attachment": []
    },
    {
        "id": 2,
        "author": "Charlotte Illidge",
        "timestamp": "2018-07-09T09:35:07+00:00",
        "note": "Hi Nick, thank you, that worked great.",
"attachment": []
    }
    ]
}
```

Listing 7-6. API/mocks/tickets/replies/10006/GET.mock

```
HTTP/1.1 200 OK
Content-Type: application/json; charset=utf-8
Access-Control-Allow-Origin: *

{
    "notes": [
        {
            "id": 1,
            "author": "James Potts",
            "timestamp": "2018-07-12T16:32:47+00:00",
            "note": "Hi there! My name is James (or Jim!) and I will be here
            to help you through this problem. <br /><br />Could you please
            let me know the last time the website was available?<br /><br /> I
            have instructed one of our engineers to look into this now and they
            are working hard to get your website back online.<br /><br /> Jim",
```

```
"attachment": []
      },
      {
        "id": 2,
        "author": "Charlotte Illidge",
        "timestamp": "2018-07-12T16:40:23+00:00",
        "note": "Hi, thank you for your quick reply.<br /><br /> The
        website has been down for about 2 hours now. <br /><br />I look
        forward to hearing back.",
"attachment": []
      }
    ]
}
```

Listings 7-7 to 7-12 include the information about each of the representatives assigned to the tickets. Add these in the same way you have added the mock files previously and follow the directory structure outlined for each listing.

Listing 7-7. API/mocks/representative-information/1/GET.mock

```
HTTP/1.1 200 OK
Content-Type: application/json; charset=utf-8
Access-Control-Allow-Origin: *

{
  "name": "James Potts",
  "role": "Senior Support Assistant",
  "bio": "I am here to help you with any support issues and to ensure you
  have a great experience, don't hesitate to ask me anything!",
  "ratingValue": 4.5
}
```

Listing 7-8. API/mocks/representative-information/2/GET.mock

```
HTTP/1.1 200 OK
Content-Type: application/json; charset=utf-8
Access-Control-Allow-Origin: *
```

```
{
  "name": "Nick Dobson",
  "role": "Account Management",
  "bio": "I am apart of the accounts team. Any issues with your account,
  such as billing, upgrades or cancellations, I am the guy to come to!",
  "ratingValue": 4.5
}
```

Listing 7-9. API/mocks/tickets/representative-information/3/GET.mock

```
HTTP/1.1 200 OK
Content-Type: application/json; charset=utf-8
Access-Control-Allow-Origin: *

{
  "name": "Oliver Butler",
  "role": "Marketing Manager",
  "bio": "I head up the marketing department here. With over 5 years
  experience, I am ready to help with any marketing or advertising
  questions you may have.",
  "ratingValue": 4
}
```

Listing 7-10. API/mocks/tickets/representative-information/4/GET.mock

```
HTTP/1.1 200 OK
Content-Type: application/json; charset=utf-8
Access-Control-Allow-Origin: *

{
  "name": "Reece Jacques",
  "role": "Data Guy",
  "bio": "I spent a long time in university studying chemistry, where
  I found a natural talent in data processing. I am responsible for
  everything data related, and happy to answer any questions!",
  "ratingValue": 4.5
}
```

Listing 7-11. API/mocks/tickets/representative-information/5/GET.mock

```
HTTP/1.1 200 OK
Content-Type: application/json; charset=utf-8
Access-Control-Allow-Origin: *

{
  "name": "Imogen Gifford",
  "role": "Content Management Expert",
  "bio": "I am an expert at content management and here to ensure your
  content experiences are as smooth as they can be.",
  "ratingValue": 4.5
}
```

Listing 7-12. API/mocks/tickets/representative-information/6/GET.mock

```
HTTP/1.1 200 OK
Content-Type: application/json; charset=utf-8
Access-Control-Allow-Origin: *

{
  "name": "Dom Ainsley",
  "role": "Domain Specialist",
  "bio": "I work as part of the domain department to help customers with
  any domain realted struggles.",
  "ratingValue": 4
}
```

List View Selections

To handle the initialization of a selected ticket, we must first add two attributes to the List View component within `ticket-desk.html`. On the `ticket-list` component created in Chapter 6, add the following attributes:

```
selection="{{selectedTicket}}"
on-selection-changed="[[listSelectionChanged]]"
```

The selection attribute will store the selected item in the list view, and the on-selection-changed attribute is an event listener that will call the listSelectionChanged function when the selection is changed. The listener is a one-way binding, as we are not expecting to write data back through this function. The selection attribute is a two-way binding, as we are expecting the selection to pass data back to the ViewModel when a user selects an item.

To store the selectedTicket, as well as the ticket model object and also the representatives ID (which is the ID of the support representative assigned to the ticket), we must create some new variables. Within the ticket desk ViewModel, add the following into the variables section:

```
self.selectedTicket = ko.observableArray([]);
self.selectedTicketModel = ko.observable();
self.selectedTicketRepId = ko.observable();
```

You will have to replace the self.ticketListDataSource() variable that was created in Chapter 6 with the following two lines of code. This will allow us to access the ticket list collection before it is passed into the CollectionTableDataSource object.

```
self.ticketList = ko.observable(ticketListCollection);
self.ticketListDataSource(new oj.CollectionTableDataSource(self.ticketList()));
```

Next, create the listSelectionChanged function shown in Listing 7-13. This function performs a few tasks. First, it assigns the selected ticket model to an observable (selectedTicketModel), by utilizing the .get method on a collection. The get method on a Collection object will return the model of the unique item ID (the idAttribute set against the Model). There is another method available too, called the .at method, which will also return a model object but instead accepts the row key rather than the ID.

The function then performs a check, to see if the selected ticket already exists within the tabData array. If it does not, it will push a new array item and bring the selected ticket into focus. If the ticket is already open, it will focus the ticket that has been selected in the list view.

Finally, the function also sets the selectedTicketRepId value, which will be used later to pass into the support representative information module.

Listing 7-13. The `listSelectionChanged` Function

```
/* List selection listener */
self.listSelectionChanged = function () {
self.selectedTicketModel(self.ticketList().get(self.selectedTicket()[0]))

        // Check if the selected ticket exists within the tab data
        var match = ko.utils.arrayFirst(self.tabData(), function
        (item) {
            return item.id == self.selectedTicket()[0];
        });

        if (!match) {
            self.tabData.push({
                "name": self.selectedTicket()[0],
                "id": self.selectedTicket()[0]
            });
        }
    self.selectedTicketRepId(self.selectedTicketModel().
    get('representativeId'));
    self.selectedTabItem(self.selectedTicket()[0]);
}
```

Now is a good time to remove the sample data from the `self.tabData` array, so that it looks like the following:

```
self.tabData = ko.observableArray([]);
```

Also remove the contents of the `selectedTabItem` variable, so that it is empty too.

```
self.selectedTabItem = ko.observable();
```

If you run the application, you should see that tabs will open as you select tickets from the list view, as illustrated in Figure 7-1.

Figure 7-1. *Working list view selection*

Extending Tab Functionality

In Chapter 6, we used the cookbook to implement an Oracle JET Tab Bar component just above where the main ticket area will go. We will now extend the tab bar further, to get the tabs functionality working with the tickets.

First, we want to make a change to the Oracle JET Tab Bar component within `ticket-desk.html` and add the following listener to the Tab Bar component. This listener will fire every time that a user clicks one of the tab items.

```
on-selection-changed="[[tabSelectionChanged]]"
```

Next, include the function from Listing 7-14 within the ViewModel. This will ensure that the selected ticket is updated when a tab is changed and also that the list view and tab are always in sync with the selected item.

Listing 7-14. The `tabSelectionChanged` Function

```
self.tabSelectionChanged = function () {
        self.selectedTicketModel(self.ticketList().get(self.selectedTabItem()))
        self.selectedTicket([self.selectedTabItem()])
}
```

Within the ViewModel, add `ojs/ojconveyorbelt` into the `define` block. Then within the `ticket-desk.html` file, wrap the entire `oj-tab-bar` element in the following component:

```
<oj-conveyor-belt class="oj-sm-9">
</oj-conveyor-belt>
```

If a user has enough tabs open that it takes up the entirety of the tab bar, the Oracle JET Conveyor Belt component will turn it into a horizontally scrollable region, making it easy for a user to scroll through all of the open tabs. Resizing the browser window with a few tabs open should show this in action.

Closing Open Tickets

To ensure that the selected ticket is reset when a tab is deleted, we will reset the selected item on both the list view and the tab bar to the first item in the index. This will prevent a scenario in which the selected item on the list view and the tab bar are in an inconsistent state. Add the following to the `deleteTab` function, directly above the `oj.Context.getContext` line.

```
/* Check if the current selected list item matches the open tab,
if so, reset to the first index in the list
*/
if(id === self.selectedTicket()[0] ||
        self.selectedTicket()[0] != self.selectedTabItem()){
        self.selectedTabItem(self.tabData()[0].id);
}
```

We also want to prevent a scenario in which there are no open tabs. To accomplish this, we will prevent the first item in the list from ever being closed. Wrap the entire contents of the `deleteTab` function in the following conditional statement:

```
// Prevent the first item in the list being removed
if(id != self.ticketList().at(0).id){
}
```

Busy Context

In the ViewModel for the ticket desk, the delete function references a class called BusyContext. This is a really useful class that can be used to get the state of any element within a JET application. In this scenario, it is used to wait for the tab bar to finish loading and then bring the list into focus.

You will find when working in JavaScript, which involves a lot of asynchronous operations, you are likely to come across scenarios in which you must wait for certain elements to finish loading before executing code that is dependent on an element to finish. BusyContext allows you to get a handle on the state of elements.

Creating the View Ticket Module

The rendering of the ticket content is going to be contained within an Oracle JET module. A module can make up a region of a page and can be dynamically replaced, as needed. We will be using a single module and changing the parameter we pass into the module to switch the content.

First, create a new View and ViewModel called view-ticket in the respective directories. (At this point, you could also delete the about, customers, and incidents modules, as they are not needed.)

Set up the view-ticket.js file, as shown in Listing 7-15.

Listing 7-15. The view-ticket.js File

```
define(['ojs/ojcore',
        'knockout',
        'jquery',
        'ojs/ojlistview',
        'ojs/ojarraydataprovider',
],
  function (oj, ko, $) {
    function ViewTicketViewModel(params) {
      var self = this;
      console.log(params.ticketModel())
    }
  return ViewTicketViewModel;
});
```

Note how we are passing `params` into the `ViewTicketViewModel` function. This parameter will be passed in when the Oracle JET module initializes.

Next, open `ticket-desk.html` and include the following directly below the tab bar (overwrite the `Ticket content goes here` text):

```
<!-- Selected Ticket View -->
<div data-bind="ojModule: { name: 'view-ticket',
                    params: {ticketModel: selectedTicketModel }
                    }" class="oj-sm-padding-4x">
</div>
<!-- Selected Ticket View -->
```

The module will pass in a parameter to the `ViewTicketViewModel`, and the parameter will be the model object of the selected ticket. After saving the file, open the web console (F12 in your browser window with the app running), and you should see an output of a `Model` object. This is the object we have passed into the view ticket ViewModel. By expanding the object, you should see the attributes of the selected ticket, as shown within Figure 7-2.

Figure 7-2. *Selected ticket* `Model` *object*

Implementing Ticket View

Within `view-ticket.js`, add the variables and computable from Listing 7-16 into the `ViewTicketViewModel` function. In this scenario, the `ticketModel` variable must be set up as a computed function in order for it to listen to the parameter changing as a user switches between tickets. When a change occurs, the computed function will update all of the observables within the module to the selected ticket information.

Listing 7-16. Variables and Computable

```
/* Variables */
self.ticketId = ko.observable();
self.title = ko.observable();
self.author = ko.observable();
self.dateCreated = ko.observable();
self.showDateDifference = ko.observable();
self.message = ko.observable();
self.status = ko.observable()
self.attachment = ko.observable();

self.ticketModel = ko.computed(function () {
        self.ticketId(params.ticketModel().get('id'))
        self.title(params.ticketModel().get('title'))
        self.author(params.ticketModel().get('author'))
        self.dateCreated(params.ticketModel().get('dateCreated'))
        self.message(params.ticketModel().get('message'))
        self.status(params.ticketModel().get('status'))
        self.attachment(params.ticketModel().get('attachment'))
        return params.ticketModel();
});
```

The `.get` method on a model object will retrieve the value of the attribute key you pass into the method.

To format the date on a ticket we require the same function (`formatDate`) that we used in Chapter 6. As we are reusing the same code, it is best to move this into a common utility file.

Create a new file under the src/js/utils folder called app-utils.js and include the contents from Listing 7-17 in that file.

Listing 7-17. The app-utils.js File

```
define(['knockout'],
    function (ko) {
        function appUtils() {
            var self = this;

        /* Utils */
        self.formatDate = function (date){
          var formatDate = oj.Validation.converterFactory(oj.
          ConverterFactory.CONVERTER_TYPE_DATETIME)
            .createConverter(
              {
                'pattern': 'dd/MM/yyyy'
              }
            );
          return formatDate.format(date)
        }

        }
        return new appUtils;
    }
)
```

Within the main.js file add the following line into the paths configuration object, which will register the library with RequireJS:

```
'appUtils': 'utils/app-utils'
```

Also, add the following object into the path_mapping.json file:

```
"appUtils": {
    "debug": {
      "src":  ["app-util.js"],
      "path": "utils/app-utils.js"
    },
```

```
    "release": {
      "src":  ["app-utils.js"],
      "path": "utils/app-utils.js"
    }
},
```

Next, import appUtils into the define block for view-ticket.js, and also ensure that you are referencing it within the parameters into the factory function too, so that you can access the methods within it. The define block for view-ticket.js should now look like the following:

```
define(['ojs/ojcore',
        'knockout',
        'jquery',
        'appUtils',
        'ojs/ojlistview',
        'ojs/ojarraydataprovider',
],
  function (oj, ko, $, appUtils)
```

Now, include the following variable declaration within view-ticket.js:

```
self.formatDate = appUtils.formatDate;
```

Note   You should go back to the ticket-desk.js file and repeat the steps of importing the appUtils library into the define block and replacing the existing formatDate function with the preceding variable.

There are a couple more functions required within view-ticket.js before we move on to the view. The first one is dateDifference (Listing 7-18), which is used to calculate the number of days between the present day and the date against the ticket, and it returns a preset string that will be displayed to the user. The second is ticketStatus (Listing 7-19), which takes the ticket status as a parameter and again returns a preset string describing the ticket status to the user.

Listing 7-18. The dateDifference Function

```javascript
/* Function to calculate date ranges */
self.dateDifference = function (date) {
     var todaysDate = new Date();
     var messageDate = new Date(date)
     var res = Math.abs(todaysDate - messageDate) / 1000;
     var days = Math.floor(res / 86400);
     if (days < 1) {
                 return "less than a day ago"
          }
          else if (days === 1) {
                 return "a day ago"
          }
          else if (days <= 7) {
                 return "less than a week ago"
          }
          else if (days > 7 && days <= 30) {
                 return "more than a week ago"
          }
          else if (days > 30) {
                 return "more than a month ago"
          }
}
```

Listing 7-19. The ticketStatus Function

```javascript
/* Function to get ticket status */
self.ticketStatus = function (status) {
                if (status === "Working") {
                   return "Ticket status currently 'working', our team are
                   hard at work looking into your issue."
                } else if (status === "Closed") {
                   return "Ticket status is 'closed', and is now in read-
                   only mode. In order to help us continue to offer the
                   best support we can, please rate your experience."
```

```
        } else if (status === "Awaiting Customer Response") {
            return "Ticket status is currently 'awaiting customer
            response', our team is awaiting your reply."
        }
    }
}
```

Open `view-ticket.html` and include the HTML markup from Listing 7-20, which is split into three parts. First, there is the ticket status, rating, and buttons. Within this section the ticket status is displayed using the preceding `ticketStatus` function, as well as some placeholder buttons for ticket management. These buttons will be implemented, along with the rating functionality, later in the book.

Second, there is the ticket header information, which is split into three columns. The first contains the avatar for the user, the second the title and the users name, and, finally, the third containing the date. Both the `formatDate` and the `dateDifference` functions are used here.

The final container outputs the message and positions it, so that it aligns with the central column of the header information. Note the use of the `html` binding instead of `text`. This is so that any HTML tags, such as line breaks, will be rendered.

Listing 7-20. HTML Markup for the `view-ticket.html` File

```
<div class="oj-flex oj-sm-padding-4x oj-sm-flex-direction-column">

    <!-- Ticket staus, rating and buttons -->
    <div class="oj-flex oj-sm-padding-2x-bottom">
        <span class="oj-sm-5 oj-sm-padding-4x-end oj-text-sm" data-
        bind="text: ticketStatus(status())"></span>
        <oj-button class="oj-flex-item oj-sm-padding-1x-end">Reply</oj-button>
        <oj-button class="oj-flex-item oj-sm-padding-1x-end">Escalate
        Priority</oj-button>
        <oj-button class="oj-flex-item oj-sm-padding-1x-end">Close Ticket
        </oj-button>
    </div>
    <!-- Ticket staus, rating and buttons -->

    <!-- Ticket header information -->
    <div class="oj-flex oj-sm-padding-4x-vertical">
```

```
        <div class="oj-sm-1 oj-sm-padding-3x-top">
            <oj-avatar role="img" aria-label="Author Avatar" size="xs">
            </oj-avatar>
        </div>

        <div class="oj-sm-8 oj-sm-flex-direction-column">
            <h2 data-bind="text: title"></h2>
            <div data-bind="text: author"></div>
        </div>

        <div class="oj-sm-2 oj-text-sm oj-sm-padding-2x-vertical">
            <div data-bind="text: dateDifference(dateCreated())"
                :title="[[formatDate(dateCreated())]]">
            </div>
        </div>

        <div class="oj-sm-1"></div>
    </div>
    <!-- Ticket header information -->

    <!-- Ticket message -->
    <div class="oj-flex oj-sm-padding-2x-vertical">
        <div class="oj-sm-1"></div>
        <div class="oj-sm-9 oj-sm-padding-4x-bottom" data-bind="html:
         message"></div>
        <div class="oj-sm-2"></div>
    </div>
    <!-- Ticket message -->
</div>
```

Running the application should output a screen similar to that shown in Figure 7-3, and clicking through the items in the list should show the different tickets.

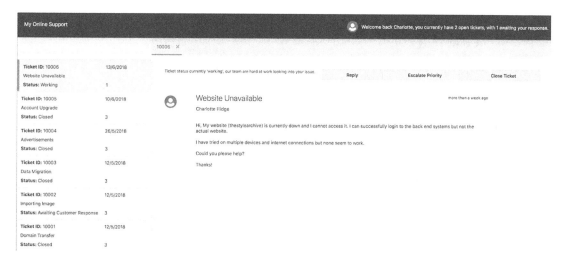

Figure 7-3. *Initial view ticket functionality*

Ticket Replies

We will be using the Oracle JET List View component again for showing the ticket replies. As outlined in the mock-ups in Chapter 3, the ticket replies alternate the positioning. The authors comments will be positioned on the left, and those of the support representative on the right. The logic for the alternation will be handled in the View.

For the ticket replies, we will be using a collection, and an API call to retrieve the replies for the selected ticket. The collection is structured differently from the one that we implemented in the previous chapter. Instead of using the standard url parameter, we are extending the oj.Collection class, so that we can build a custom URL (Listing 7-21). The custom URL attibute is needed as we will be appending the ticket ID to the service end point.

Listing 7-21. Ticket Replies Model and Collection

```
/* List View Collection and Model */
self.ticketRepliesDataSource = ko.observable();
self.ticketReplyModel = oj.Model.extend({
  idAttribute: 'id'
});

var ticketRepliesCollection = oj.Collection.extend({
  customURL: function () {
    var retObj = {};
```

```
      retObj['url'] = "http://localhost:8080/tickets/replies/" + self.
      ticketId()
      return retObj
    },
    model: self.ticketReplyModel
  });

  self.ticketReplies = new ticketRepliesCollection();
  self.ticketRepliesDataSource(new oj.CollectionTableDataSource(self.
  ticketReplies));

  self.ticketId.subscribe(function(){
    self.ticketReplies.fetch();
  })
```

Within the View below the ticket message, add the List View component and its template (Listing 7-22). The css and style bindings are being used in the template to alternate the positioning of the tickets. We are able to check if the comment is from the original author, and then use the flex-direction attribute to specify the direction of the flex-items.

Listing 7-22. List View Component and Template

```
<!-- List to render ticket replies -->
    <oj-list-view
        id="reply-list-view"
        aria-label="ticket reply list"
        class="oj-sm-12"
        data="[[ticketRepliesDataSource]]"
      item.renderer="[[oj.KnockoutTemplateUtils.getRenderer('ticket-replies-
      template', true)]]">
    </oj-list-view>
    <!-- List to render ticket replies -->

    <!-- List Template -->
    <script type="text/html" id="ticket-replies-template">
        <li data-bind="attr: {id: $data['id']}">
```

```
<!-- First row of list item, sets up the item header -->
<div class="oj-flex oj-sm-padding-4x-vertical"
    data-bind="style: { flexDirection: author !== $parent.
    author() ? 'row-reverse' : " }">

    <div class="oj-flex-item oj-sm-1 oj-sm-padding-2x-top"
        data-bind="css: author !== $parent.author() ?
        'oj-sm-padding-4x-start' : 'oj-sm-padding-4x-end'">
        <oj-avatar
            role="img"
            aria-label="User Avatar"
            size="xs">
        </oj-avatar>
    </div>

    <div class="oj-sm-8 oj-sm-flex-direction-column">
        <h2 data-bind="text: 'RE: ' + $parent.title(),
                        style: { textAlign: author !== $parent.
                        author() ? 'right' : " }">
        </h2>
        <div data-bind="text: author,
                        style: { textAlign: author !== $parent.
                        author() ? 'right' : " }">
        </div>
    </div>

    <div class="oj-sm-2 oj-text-sm oj-sm-padding-2x-vertical">
        <div
            data-bind="text: $parent.dateDifference(timestamp)"
            :title="[[$parent.formatDate(timestamp)]]">
        </div>
    </div>

    <div class="oj-sm-1">
    </div>
</div>
```

```
        <!-- Second row in list item, outputs the message content -->
        <div class="oj-flex oj-sm-padding-2x-vertical">
            <div class="oj-sm-1"></div>
            <div class="oj-sm-10 oj-sm-padding-4x-bottom"
                data-bind="html: note"></div>
            <div class="oj-sm-1"></div>
        </div>
    </li>
</script>
<!-- List Template -->
```

Tidying Up and Styling

There are a few extra tweaks we can make to tidy up the design of the view ticket and replies. First, there is a hover background on list view items. Let's remove this, so that you don't get a hover background on ticket replies. Add the following into the list-view SASS partial:

```
.oj-listview {
    .oj-hover {
        background-color: transparent;
    }
}
```

Next, add a height to the view ticket container, to keep everything nicely aligned. Add the following class to the containers partial, which will calculate the height and uses overflow-y to apply a scrollbar vertically only:

```
.view-ticket-container {
    height: calc(100vh - 161px);
    overflow-y: scroll
}
```

Then add the following placeholder class for the support representative area that we will create in the next section, also in the containers partial.

```
.support-rep-container {
    background-color: $neutral-color;
}
```

Finally, the `Selected Ticket View` section within the `ticket-desk.html` file should be replaced with the following, to include the new classes and a new div placeholder for the support representatives:

```
<!-- Selected Ticket View -->
    <div class="oj-flex">
      <div class="oj-sm-9 view-ticket-container">
        <div data-bind="ojModule: { name: 'view-ticket',
                params: {ticketModel: selectedTicketModel}
                }" class="oj-sm-padding-4x">
        </div>
      </div>
      <div class="oj-sm-3 support-rep-container"></div>
    </div>
<!-- Selected Ticket View -->
```

The expected outcome is illustrated in Figure 7-4.

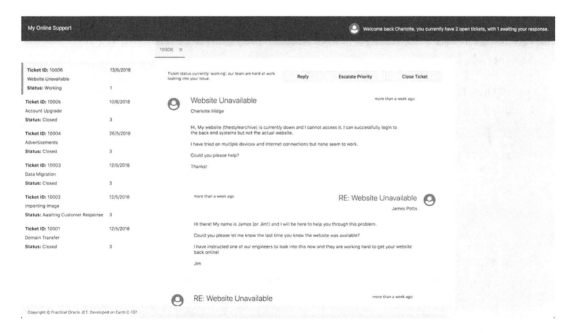

Figure 7-4. *Ticket view with comments*

Support Representative

We will now include one more Oracle JET module, which will be responsible for displaying information about the support representative. Create a new View and ViewModel called `view-representative`. Within the ViewModel, include the code from Listing 7-23.

Similar to the view ticket module, the new module will also have a parameter (`repId` in this case) passed in. This `repId` is then used when calling the `representative-information` end point. The Oracle JET Gauge (ojGauge) UI component is imported here, as it will be used for the representatives rating.

Listing 7-23. Code to Display Information About the Representative

```
define(['ojs/ojcore',
        'knockout',
        'jquery',
        'ojs/ojgauge'],

  function (oj, ko, $) {
    function RepresentativeViewModel(params) {
      var self = this;

      self.name = ko.observable();
      self.role = ko.observable();
      self.bio = ko.observable()
      self.ratingValue = ko.observable();

      self.repId = ko.computed(function () {
        return params.repId;
      });

      $.ajax({
        type: "GET",
        url: "http://localhost:8080/representative-information/" + self.repId(),
        crossDomain: true,
        success: function (res) {
            self.name(res.name)
            self.role(res.role)
```

```
                self.bio(res.bio)
                self.ratingValue(res.ratingValue)
            },
            error: function (jqXHR, textStatus, errorThrown) {
                console.error(jqXHR)
            }
        });

    }
    return RepresentativeViewModel;
  }
);
```

Add the code from Listing 7-24 into the view. The Gauge component takes in a numeric value from 1 to 5, and the selected-state.color attribute sets the color of the stars. This gauge is read-only.

Listing 7-24. Representative View

```
<div class="oj-flex oj-sm-flex-direction-column oj-sm-align-items-center
oj-sm-padding-4x">
        <oj-avatar role="img" aria-label="Representative Avatar"
        size="md"></oj-avatar>
        <span data-bind="text: name" class="oj-sm-padding-2x-vertical"></span>
        <strong data-bind="text: role" class="oj-sm-padding-2x-vertical"></strong>
        <span data-bind="text: bio" class="oj-sm-padding-2x-vertical"></span>

        <span class="oj-sm-padding-4x-top">Average Rating</span>
        <oj-rating-gauge
            id="ticket-rating"
            value="[[ratingValue]]"
            readonly
            selected-state.color="#E74C3C"
            style="width:120px;height:25px;">
        </oj-rating-gauge>
</div>
```

Finally, within with ticket desk View, add the following module into the support-rep-container div that we added in the previous section.

```
<div data-bind="ojModule: {
        name: 'view-representative',
        params: { repId: selectedTicketRepId() }
        }" class="oj-sm-padding-4x">
</div>
```

The final output from this chapter should look like Figure 7-5 and contain the functionality to navigate all tickets and see all the information about them.

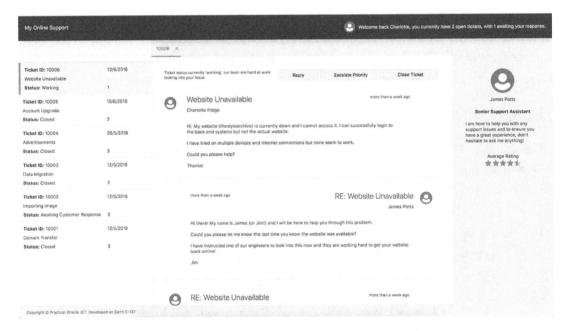

Figure 7-5. *Chapter 7 expected outcome*

Summary

Chapter 7 has taken you from having an application that was in its infancy to one that is suddenly starting to take shape and demonstrates a read-only view of all the tickets. A number of new components have been used, and the addition of a utility file shows how easy it can be to move common functions into utility files that can be reused across an application.

Passing parameters through to components and tracking any changes to the parameters has also been used, which is really important when breaking an application into smaller chunks, ensuring that the right data is passed between them.

Finally, we extended the tabs components to open the correct tickets and keep the state of the open tickets between the list view.

CHAPTER 8

Replying to Tickets

A common requirement of an application is to provide a user with the ability to input longer portions of text. Unfortunately, in many cases, a standard HTML text area will not meet that requirement, as richer functionality is needed. Even a simple line break will mean looking elsewhere for a richer text editor.

In this chapter, we are going to use a text editor called Trumbowyg, which is a lightweight What You See Is What You Get (WYSIWYG) editor. The editor comes with a lot of great features, but we are mainly using it to offer line breaks and a few extra formatting options to the user.

You can find more information about the editor at its web site: `https://alex-d.github.io/Trumbowyg/`.

In this chapter, the following elements and classes will be used:

- *ojModule*
- *ojCollection*
- *ojButton*
- *ojFilePicker*
- *ojBindIf*
- *Trumbowyg* (third-party library)
- *FontAwesome* (third-party library)

API Setup

This chapter will include some new API requests when posting a ticket reply. Therefore, some new mock files must be created. The POST requests won't be doing anything other than returning a successful response. Therefore, we can use the same file for all ticket IDs. The `mockserver` plug-in has a wildcard function, and by creating a directory with two underscores (__), `mockserver` will match any requests, for any ticket ID.

141

© Daniel Curtis 2019
D. Curtis, *Practical Oracle JET*, https://doi.org/10.1007/978-1-4842-4346-6_8

Listings 8-1 and 8-2 are the mocks for ticket replies. Add these in the same way you have added the mock files previously and follow the directory structure outlined for each listing.

Listing 8-1. API/mocks/tickets/replies/__/OPTIONS.mock

```
HTTP/1.1 200 OK
Content-Type: application/json; charset=utf-8
Access-Control-Allow-Origin: *
Access-Control-Allow-Headers: Origin, X-Requested-With, Content-Type, Accept
```

Listing 8-2. API/mocks/tickets/replies/__/POST.mock

```
HTTP/1.1 200 OK
Content-Type: application/json; charset=utf-8
Access-Control-Allow-Origin: *
Access-Control-Allow-Headers: Origin, X-Requested-With, Content-Type, Accept
Access-Control-Allow-Methods: GET, POST, PUT

{}
```

We will also need to create a successful response for a file upload. Add Listing 8-3 to the directory structure listed.

Listing 8-3. API/mocks/tickets/upload/__/POST.mock

```
HTTP/1.1 200 OK
Content-Type: application/json; charset=utf-8
Access-Control-Allow-Origin: *
Access-Control-Allow-Headers: Origin, X-Requested-With, Content-Type, Accept
Access-Control-Allow-Methods: GET, POST, PUT

{}
```

Setting Up

To begin, make sure that you have the *trumbowyg* library installed. You should have installed this in Chapter 4, but here is a reminder of how to add it. First, run the following command in your UI directory:

```
npm install trumbowyg
```

Then add Listing 8-4 into the path_mappings.json file, so that the Oracle JET tooling will copy over all the files required during build.

Listing 8-4. trumbowyg Setup

```
"trumbowyg": {
     "cdn": "3rdparty",
     "cwd": "node_modules/trumbowyg/dist",
     "debug": {
       "src":  ["trumbowyg.min.js", "ui/icons.svg", "plugins/cleanpaste/**"],
       "path": "libs/trumbowyg/trumbowyg.min.js"
     },
     "release": {
       "src":  ["trumbowyg.min.js", "ui/icons.svg", "plugins/cleanpaste/**"],
       "path": "libs/trumbowyg/trumbowyg.min.js"
     }
},
```

Include the library reference within the configuration block in main.js.

```
'trumbowyg': '',
```

Finally, make sure that the library import is included within the define block for view-ticket.js.

Copying over the CSS

The trumbowyg library requires some CSS classes to render. We can use the oraclejet-build.js tooling file explored in Chapter 4 to copy over the CSS into the theme mosTheme. First, create a new directory in the theme called third-party (src/themes/mosTheme/web/third-party).

Next, navigate to scripts/config and open oraclejet-build.js. Within this file, navigate to the sass section and replace the commented out sass object with Listing 8-5.

Listing 8-5. sass Object within `oraclejet-build.js`

```
sass: {
        fileList: [
            {
                cwd: 'node_modules/trumbowyg/dist/ui/sass',
                src: ['*'],
                dest: 'src/themes/mosTheme/web/third-party'
            }
        ],
        options: {}
},
```

The code in Listing 8-5 will copy over the contents of the sass directory within the
trumbowyg installation folder into the new third-party folder created within the theme.
It will also compile the SASS into CSS.

Finally, import the third-party/trumbowyg.css file in the mosTheme.scss file, as
shown in Figure 8-1.

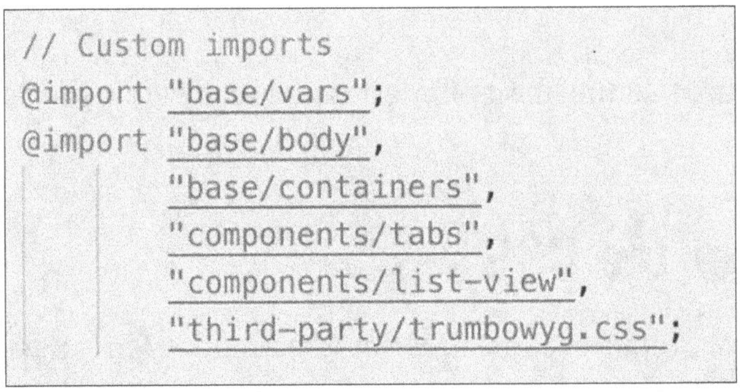

```
// Custom imports
@import "base/vars";
@import "base/body",
        "base/containers",
        "components/tabs",
        "components/list-view",
        "third-party/trumbowyg.css";
```

Figure 8-1. *Importing third-party CSS*

Initializing the Editor

Within view-ticket.html, add the following elements below the list template at the
bottom of the file (but ensure that they are still within the container div):

```
<h3 class="oj-sm-padding-4x">Reply</h3>
<div id="ticket-reply-area"></div>
```

Now, add `trumbowyg` to the end of the `define` block, within the `view-ticket.js` file. You do not have to pass this into the callback function.

The div we created previously with the ID of `ticket-reply-area` will be replaced with the `trumbowyg` editor, once we initialize it. Initializing the editor is straightforward. You hook onto the `ticket-reply-area` and call the `trumbowyg` method, as follows:

```
$('#ticket-reply-area').trumbowyg()
```

However, if you include the preceding within the ViewModel and serve the application, you will notice that it does not work, as the element will not be present in the DOM at the time that it is trying to initialize. To understand this further, we must look at the ojModule life cycle.

The ojModule binding comes with some listeners that provide the ability to execute code at different points in the module's life cycle. There are eight of these listeners in total, and it is useful to understand what they are and how they can be used. Here's the rundown:

1. `handleAttached`: Will run after the View has been inserted into the DOM

2. `handleActivated`: Will run before the View is about to use the ViewModel. It is typically used to fetch data before the View transitions.

3. `handleBindingsApplied`: Will run after the bindings have been applied to the View. Note that if the current view is retrieved from the cache, the bindings will not be reapplied, and the function will not be run.

4. `handleDeactivated`: Will run after the View and ViewModel become inactive, when everything has been run and there is no more user interaction

5. `handleDetached`: Will run after the View is removed from the DOM

6. `handleTransitionCompleted`: Will run after a View transitions, and any animation between the old and new view is complete

7. `Dispose`: Will run before module is destroyed. Should be used to perform any clean-up tasks

8. `Initialize`: Will run when the ViewModel is created (but not when it is retrieved from the cache). It will also run only when the ViewModel is returned as an instance, rather than a constructor function.

Note   Oracle JET currently offers both an Oracle JET Module Component (which is used in the `index.html` file to load the router modules) and an ojModule binding (or namespace). Here, we are working with the ojModule binding and using it instead of the component, as it has more support for the functionality we are trying to achieve. The two module variations have different life cycle methods, so make sure not to get them confused.

The life cycle event that we need to initialize the editor is going to be `handleAttached`. This is because all we are waiting on is for the DOM to finish loading and the div that we need to latch on to being present. Therefore, at this point in the life cycle, the element will be present.

To implement the listener and activate the editor, add the following into the `view-ticket.js` file:

```
self.handleAttached = function () {
        $('#ticket-reply-area').trumbowyg()
};
```

It is possible to restrict the options a user has access to and apply options that are not available by default. If you were working with a system that had different user roles, you would be able to initialize the editor with different available options, by checking the user's roles and then altering the buttons or parameters available to that role.

The `resetCss` parameter prevents any page CSS interfering with the editor, and the `removeformatPasted` parameter prevents any pasted formatting from being applied.

Expand the editor initialization by including the options shown in Listing 8-6.

Listing 8-6. Initialize Editor with Options

```
self.handleAttached = function () {
        $('#ticket-reply-area').trumbowyg(
                {
```

```
            btns: ['bold', 'italic', 'underline'],
            resetCss: true,
            removeformatPasted: true
        }
    );
}
```

If you now rebuild and serve the application, you should see the editor initialized, and you should be able to type into the editor and use the formatting options, as illustrated in Figure 8-2.

Figure 8-2. *Ticket reply editor initialized*

File Picker

To allow users to add attachments onto replies, we will be using the Oracle JET File Picker component. Import the file picker component (`ojs/ojfilepicker`) into the define block within `view-ticket.js`.

The file picker component will use the following attributes:

- `on-oj-selected`: References a function to call when a user has selected a file

- `accept`: An array of accepted file types

- `selection-mode`: Specifies whether the picker allows single or multiple file uploads in one go. We are allowing single only.

The Oracle JET `flex-bar` classes will be used to position the file upload and reply buttons to the start and the end of the container. Flex bar has the following classes available:

- `oj-flex-bar-start`: Class for the start section; will resize to the size of the content

- `oj-flex-bar-end`: Class for the end section; will resize to the size of the content

- `oj-flex-bar-middle`: Class for the middle section; will stretch to meet the start and end

An Oracle JET BindText component is used to bind the file name to the view. This component has only a single attribute of `value`, and the component is removed from the DOM after the bindings have been applied.

The ojBindIf component is used to check if a file has been uploaded before initializing the ojBindText.

Under the text editor, include the code from Listing 8-7.

Listing 8-7. File Picker and Ticket Reply Button

```
<div class="oj-flex-bar">
    <div class="oj-flex-bar-start oj-sm-align-items-center">
        <oj-file-picker class='oj-filepicker-custom oj-sm-padding-2x-end'
            id="fileUpload"
            selectOn='click'
            on-oj-select='[[fileSelectionListener]]'
            accept="[[allowedFileTypes]]"
            selection-mode='single'>
            <oj-button slot='trigger'>
```

```
            <span slot='startIcon' class='oj-fwk-icon oj-fwk-icon-
              arrowbox-n'></span>
                    Upload
                </oj-button>
            </oj-file-picker>
            <oj-bind-if test='[[uploadedFile()[0]]]'>
                <oj-bind-text value="[[uploadedFile()[0].name]]"></oj-bind-
                  text>
            </oj-bind-if>
        </div>
        <div class="oj-flex-bar-end">
            <oj-button id='reply-button' on-oj-action='[[ticketReply]]'>Reply
            </oj-button>
        </div>
    </div>
</div>
```

Then create two new variables to hold the selected file and the allowed file types. Add these into the variable section of the view-ticket ViewModel.

```
self.uploadedFile = ko.observableArray([]);
self.allowedFileTypes = ko.observableArray(['image/*']);
```

Add the fileSelectionListener and a placeholder ticketReply function. (We will add to this in the next section.) The listener will assign the selected file the uploadedFile variable.

```
self.fileSelectionListener = function(event){
        var file = event.detail.files;
        self.uploadedFile(file)
}
self.ticketReply = function (){
}
```

Make sure that the application is running and check that the new file picker and flex bar look similar to those in Figure 8-3.

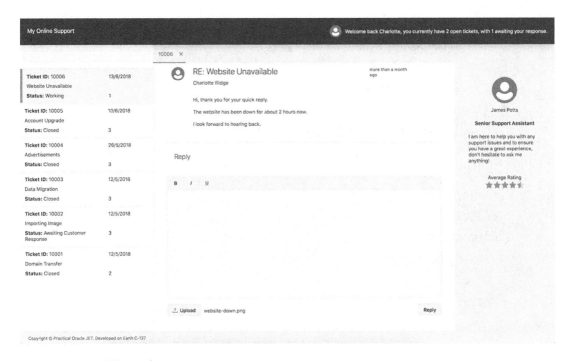

Figure 8-3. *File picker*

Sending the Reply

Even though there is no data is being sent to a database, it is still possible to handle the reply and apply it to the collection locally. To process ticket replies, we must create an object of the reply data and use the collection methods to create a new record.

A separate function will be created to handle sending uploaded attachments to the server. The upload request will use a promise, as we will be handling two requests being initiated in the same action. A promise is needed to wait for the file to be uploaded before applying a new model to the collection.

What Is a Promise?

You may have heard the term *callback* when working with JavaScript. A callback function is a function that is executed when another function has finished executing. This is common across all JavaScript applications, owing to JavaScript's asynchronous non-blocking I/O model. The model means that operations (AJAX calls) can occur in parallel to the application code running.

Therefore, when waiting for an asynchronous response, any code that is dependent on that response must be placed in a callback function, which will be called after the result is returned. This works well when you have one callback but can get messy when you have multiple callbacks and end up in what is known as "callback hell."

Promises were formally introduced in ES6, and they are essentially an object that contains an asynchronous task. The promise will notify the user when the task has finished, with information about the result.

As the reply action can potentially send out two asynchronous requests, a promise will be required in order for the first request to wait for the result before the second request is called.

Creating a Promise

Let's create the promise to upload a file. The promise will call the upload API and return a resolve message, if the service call is successful, or a reject message, if not. Add Listing 8-8 into the view-ticket ViewModel.

Listing 8-8. uploadFile Function

```
/* Promise to call the file upload function */
self.uploadFile = function () {
        return new Promise(
            function (resolve, reject) {
                var file = $( "#fileUpload" ).find( "input" )[0].files[0];
                var data = new FormData();
                data.append("file", file);
                $.ajax({
                    type: "POST",
                    url: "http://localhost:8080/tickets/upload/" +
                    self.ticketId(),
                    contentType: false,
                    processData: false,
                    data: data,
                    success: function (result) {
                        resolve("success")
                        console.log("File uploaded successfully!");
```

```
            },
            error: function (err, status, errorThrown) {
                reject(err);
                console.error("Error")
            }
        });
    }
)
}
```

Next, update the empty `ticketReply` function, as shown in Listing 8-9. The function will check if a file has been selected by the user. If it has, it calls the promise and specifies the actions to run if the promise resolves.

Listing 8-9. `ticketReply` Function

```
self.ticketReply = function() {
        var date = new Date();
        var attachment = [];

        if(self.uploadedFile()[0] != null){
            self.uploadFile()
            .then(function (success){
                attachment =  [{
                    "filePath": self.uploadedFile()[0].name,
                    "fileSize": bytesToSize(self.uploadedFile()[0].size),
                    "timestamp": date.toISOString(),
                }]

                self.addTicketReplytoCollection(attachment, date);
            })
            .catch(function(error){
                console.error('Error uploading file')
            })
        } else {
            self.addTicketReplytoCollection(attachment, date);
        }
}
```

Add the following utility function, to convert the bytes into a file size:

```
/* Function to convert bytes to size
Source: http://codeaid.net/javascript/convert-size-in-bytes-to-human-
readable-format-(javascript)#comment-1
*/
function bytesToSize(bytes) {
                var sizes = ['Bytes', 'KB', 'MB', 'GB', 'TB'];
                if (bytes == 0) return 'n/a';
                var i = parseInt(Math.floor(Math.log(bytes) / Math.log(1024)));
                return Math.round(bytes / Math.pow(1024, i), 2) + ' ' + sizes[i];
};
```

Now we must create the function addTicketReplytoCollection from Listing 8-10. This function is responsible for adding the new reply to the ticketReplies collection using the create method on an ojCollection. The create method will add a new model to the collection and call the data service.

Getting the value (or HTML) from the Trumbowyg editor is achieved by initializing the .trumbowyg method on the element and passing in html as the parameter.

Note   The wait:true parameter in the create method. This is quite an important parameter to add when working with collections. It prevents the new item from being added to the local collection until a successful response has been received from the data service. If the API call fails but the model is added locally, the application could be in an inconsistent state.

Listing 8-10. addTicketReplytoCollection Function

```
/* Function to build up the ticket reply and add it to the collection */
self.addTicketReplytoCollection = function(attachment, date){
                var newReply = {
                    "author": "Charlotte Illidge",
                    "timestamp": date.toISOString(),
                    "note": $('#ticket-reply-area').trumbowyg('html'),
                    "attachment": attachment
                }
```

```
self.ticketReplies.create(newReply, {
    wait: true,
    success: function(model, response, options){
        console.log("Success")
    },
    error: function(err, status, errorThrown){
        console.error("Error")
    }
})

$('#ticket-reply-area').trumbowyg('empty');
self.uploadedFile('');
}
```

Update the ticketReplyModel function to include the customURL attribute, as shown in Listing 8-11. This is required, so the model knows which end point to call when adding a new item.

Listing 8-11. Updated ticketReplyModel

```
self.ticketReplyModel = oj.Model.extend({
        idAttribute: 'id',
        customURL: function () {
            var retObj = {};
            retObj['url'] = "http://localhost:8080/tickets/replies/" +
            self.ticketId()
            return retObj
        }
});
```

Finally, to ensure that the contents of the editor and any selected file is cleared when switching between tickets, add the following into the subscribe method for ticketId:

```
$('#ticket-reply-area').trumbowyg('empty');
self.uploadedFile('');
```

If you now serve the application, you should be able to type a reply into the text area, and upon submit, the response will appear straightaway, as shown in Figure 8-4.

Figure 8-4. Ticket reply

Reply Toolbar Button

In the button toolbar at the top of the ticket, there is a reply button. The purpose of this button is to navigate users to the reply editor, to prevent them having to scroll in cases of long tickets. First, add the on-oj-action attribute to the reply button component in the view-ticket.html file, which should call a scrollToReply function when a user clicks the button. Then add the scrollToReply function in the view-ticket.js file and use the scrollIntoView JavaScript method on the ticket reply area element.

```
<oj-button class="oj-flex-item oj-sm-padding-1x-end" on-oj-
action='[[scrollToReply]]'>Reply</oj-button>
```

```
/* Function to automatically scroll the user to the reply editor */
    self.scrollToReply = function(){
        document.getElementById('ticket-reply-area').scrollIntoView();
}
```

Installing FontAwesome

In the next section, we are going to show file attachments within tickets. Before we do that, we will install a new library called FontAwesome. Until now, the application has used a default icon set that comes bundled with Oracle JET. This icon set is limited, so we must install a third-party library to get the icons we need.

First, install the FontAwesome library by running the following command in the UI directory: `npm install @fontawesome/fontawesome-free`.

Then we must copy FontAwesome into the project, by using the copyCustomLibsToStaging build task. Open `oraclejet-build.js` and replace the commented out copyCustomLibsToStaging object with Listing 8-12.

Listing 8-12. copyCustomLibsToStaging Object

```
copyCustomLibsToStaging: {
    fileList: [
      {
          cwd: 'node_modules/@fortawesome/fontawesome-free/',
          src: ['css/*', 'webfonts/*'],
          dest: 'web/css/fontawesome'
      }
    ]
},
```

Then include the style sheet within head of the `index.html` file.

```
<!-- This contains the fontawesome import -->
<link rel="stylesheet" href="css/fontawesome/css/all.css" type="text/css"/>
```

If you rebuild the application, you will notice the fontawesome directory appear in web/css, as illustrated in Figure 8-5.

Figure 8-5. *FontAwesome library*

Displaying File Attachments

As it is possible for tickets and their replies to contain attachments, we must add the display logic to show these.

Within `view-ticket.html`, add Listing 8-13 directly below the ticket author's name.

Listing 8-13. File Attachment Display

```
<oj-bind-if test='[[attachment()[0]]]'>
            <div class="oj-flex oj-sm-padding-2x-top">
                <span class="fas fa-paperclip"></span>
                <div class="oj-sm-padding-1x-horizontal" data-
                  bind="text: attachment()[0].filePath"></div>
                (<div data-bind="text: attachment()[0].fileSize"></div>)
            </div>
</oj-bind-if>
```

The ojBindIf component checks whether there are any attachments associated with this ticket, and if there are, show the attachment. The span element contains the classes `fas fa-paperclip`, which will load the paperclip FontAwesome icon. A full list of available classes and icons is available on the FontAwesome web site.

Users can also add attachments to ticket replies. Therefore, the attachment display logic has to be added to the replies list. The code for this is similar; only the binding references are different. Add Listing 8-14 into the `ticket-replies-template` and again below the author name.

Listing 8-14. File Attachment Display for Replies

```
<oj-bind-if test='[[attachment[0]]]'>
                    <div class="oj-flex oj-sm-padding-2x-top" data-
                    bind="style: { textAlign: author !== $parent.
                    author() ? 'right' : '' }">
                        <span class="fas fa-paperclip"></span>
                        <div class="oj-sm-padding-1x-horizontal" data-
                        bind="text: attachment[0].filePath"></div>
                        (<div data-bind="text: attachment[0].
                        fileSize"></div>)
                    </div>
</oj-bind-if>
```

An example of how attachments are displayed on tickets can be seen in Figure 8-6.

Figure 8-6. *Ticket with attachment*

Adding Icons to Buttons

It is possible to add icons to buttons, by using component functionality called 'slots'. A slot can be used to insert code into a component at certain positions. In this example, we can use the `startIcon` slot to include an icon within the button component.

Within the upload button, replace the existing slot icon (which is an Oracle JET icon) with a FontAwesome icon.

```
<span slot='startIcon' class='fas fa-upload'></span>
```

Then add in a slot for the reply button.

```
<span slot='startIcon' class='fas fa-reply'></span>
```

The buttons should then look like the buttons within Figure 8-7.

Figure 8-7. *Buttons with FontAwesome icons*

Summary

After completing this chapter, the application will now be more interactive. You have installed a third-party library to render a WYSIWYG editor and learned the module life cycle methods. You have also used the Oracle JET Collection `create` method to add a new ticket reply, as well as implementing a promise to handle asynchronous responses.

You have used the Oracle JET File Picker component to select a file and send it to the server and displayed the file picker and reply button, using the CSS flex-bar classes. Finally, you will have included the FontAwesome library and applied some of the icons on the tickets.

CHAPTER 9

Ticket Management

This chapter walks through the creation of management tasks that can be performed on a ticket. These include ticket closure, escalating priority, and rating responses. The buttons that will action these management tasks are situated within the view ticket module, and any actions on these buttons will be communicated to the parent module (ticket desk), in order to perform methods directly on the ticket's model and collection.

To handle this communication, we are going to look at JS signals. Within the `main.js` file, you may have already noticed that there is a library included called `js-signals`, as shown in Figure 9-1. The signals library comes bundled with every new Oracle JET application and is used as a way of managing events between Oracle JET modules.

```
// Path mappings for the logical module names
// Update the main-release-paths.json for release mode when upd
paths:
//injector:mainReleasePaths
{
  'knockout': 'libs/knockout/knockout-3.4.2.debug',
  'jquery': 'libs/jquery/jquery-3.3.1',
  'jqueryui-amd': 'libs/jquery/jqueryui-amd-1.12.1',
  'promise': 'libs/es6-promise/es6-promise',
  'hammerjs': 'libs/hammer/hammer-2.0.8',
  'ojdnd': 'libs/dnd-polyfill/dnd-polyfill-1.0.0',
  'ojs': 'libs/oj/v5.0.0/debug',
  'ojL10n': 'libs/oj/v5.0.0/ojL10n',
  'ojtranslations': 'libs/oj/v5.0.0/resources',
  'text': 'libs/require/text',
  'signals': 'libs/js-signals/signals',
  'customElements': 'libs/webcomponents/custom-elements.min',
  'proj4': 'libs/proj4js/dist/proj4-src',
  'css': 'libs/require-css/css',
  'appUtils': 'utils/appUtils',
  'trumbowyg': 'libs/trumbowyg/trumbowyg.min'
}
//endinjector
```

Figure 9-1. *Signals import*

API Setup

This chapter will introduce some new API requests when closing and escalating a ticket. Therefore, some new mock files must be created.

Just as you have done in previous chapters, create the two mock files shown in Listings 9-1 and 9-2. These two listings use the wildcard feature (__) of mockserver to capture any PUT requests for all the tickets.

Listing 9-1. `API/mocks/tickets/__/OPTIONS.mock`

```
HTTP/1.1 200 OK
Content-Type: application/json; charset=utf-8
Access-Control-Allow-Origin: *
Access-Control-Allow-Headers: Origin, X-Requested-With, Content-Type,
Accept
Access-Control-Allow-Methods: GET, POST, PUT
```

Listing 9-2. `API/mocks/tickets/__/PUT.mock`

```
HTTP/1.1 200 OK
Content-Type: application/json; charset=utf-8
Access-Control-Allow-Origin: *

[]
```

Understanding Signals

Events outline something that has happened on an HTML element. An event can be the result of a user action (e.g., clicking a button) or something the browser has done (e.g., finished loading a page). It is possible to create and listen to custom events, using the JavaScript event dispatch/listener system. A new event can be created with a custom string-based identifier that can be picked up by a listener elsewhere in the application.

Signals are similar to events, except that signals have a central controller. This use of a central controller has the benefit of not relying on string-based event listeners scattered across the application that could be incorrectly spelled. Signals accept multiple parameters being passed into the central controller when dispatching, whereas events accept only a single parameter.

The purpose of signals is to communicate between different modules, and in this case, we will be sending signals from the view ticket module to the parent ticket desk module. These signals will inform the ticket desk module of any changes to tickets (if they are closed, or if they have had their priority escalated).

The js-signal library comes with several methods that are described in the following subsections. Not all methods are described, only the more commonly used ones.

add

The add method will add a listener to the signal object and accepts three parameters:

1. Listener: The function that will be executed once the listener detects a dispatch signal

2. ListenerContext: An optional parameter that specifies the context in which the listener will be executed

3. Priority: An optional parameter that specifies the priority of the listener. The higher the priority, the higher up the order the listener will be executed. The default value is zero.

Note Use addOnce instead of add, if you want to remove the listener after the first execution.

---

dispatch

The dispatch method is used to broadcast a signal to all listeners. It allows for multiple parameters to be passed in, but parameters are not required.

dispose

Invoking the dispose method destroys the signal object. Calling any method on the instance following a dispose will cause errors.

remove

Call the remove method to remove a listener. The listener to remove should be passed as a parameter. Use removeAll to remove all listeners.

Ticket Closure and Priority Update

Before we begin, you must include the signals library within the `define` block in both the `ticket-desk` and `view-ticket` ViewModels. Then make sure that the signals library is also passed into the callback function. As an example, the start of the `ticket-desk.js` should look like the following:

```
define(['ojs/ojcore',
'knockout',
'jquery',
'appUtils',
'signals',
'ojs/ojlistview',
'ojs/ojinputtext',
'ojs/ojcollectiontabledatasource',
'ojs/ojmodel',
'ojs/ojvalidation-datetime',
'ojs/ojconveyorbelt'],
function(oj, ko, $, appUtils, signals) {
```

We will be setting up two signals: one for ticket closures and another for updating the ticket priority. Both signal controllers should be added to the variables section in `ticket-desk.js`. For example:

```
self.closeTicketSignal = new signals.Signal();
self.updatePrioritySignal = new signals.Signal();
```

Next, update the parameters being passed into the view ticket module so that the signals are shared with the view ticket module. The module binding within ticket-desk. html should look as follows:

```
<div data-bind="ojModule: { name: 'view-ticket',
                params: {ticketModel: selectedTicketModel,
closeTicketSignal: closeTicketSignal, updatePrioritySignal:
updatePrioritySignal}
                }" class="oj-sm-padding-4x">
</div>
```

Within `view-ticket.js`, assign the signal parameters to variables and create a new `priority` observable to store the tickets' priority. The `closureReason` variable is also needed, to hold the reason for ticket closures.

```
self.closeTicketSignal = params.closeTicketSignal;
self.updatePrioritySignal = params.updatePrioritySignal;
self.priority = ko.observable();
self.closureReason = ko.observable();
```

Ensure that the priority observable is populated when the ticket is loaded. Do that by adding the following to the `ticketModel` computed function:

```
self.priority(params.ticketModel().get('priority'));
```

Create the functions from Listing 9-3. The `closeTicket` and `escalatePriority` functions will initialize the `dispatch` method on the respective signals. The dialog functions are used to handle the interaction, with a confirmation dialog created within the next section.

Listing 9-3. Closure and Escalation Functions

```
/* Functions to close a ticket via a signal to the ticket desk VM */
self.confirmCloseDialog = function (event) {
    document.getElementById('close-confirmation-dialog').open();
}

self.closeDialog = function (event) {
    document.getElementById('close-confirmation-dialog').close();
}

self.closeTicket = function() {
    self.closeTicketSignal.dispatch(self.ticketId(),
    self.closureReason());
    self.closeDialog();
}
```

```
/* Function to escalate a ticket via a signal to the ticket desk VM */
self.escalatePriority = function() {
        // Only send the signal if the priority is lower than 1
        if(self.priority() > 1){
            self.updatePrioritySignal.dispatch(self.ticketId());
        }
}
```

Update the buttons within `view-ticket.html` to include a FontAwesome icon and `oj-action` events. Ensure that the disabled attribute is set on the Escalate Priority button. This will disable the button if the priority of the ticket is already at its highest (which is 1). Listing 9-4 shows how these buttons should now look.

Listing 9-4. Updated Ticket Management Buttons

```
<oj-button
        class="oj-flex-item oj-sm-padding-1x-end"
        on-oj-action='[[scrollToReply]]'>
        <span slot='startIcon' class='fas fa-reply'></span>
        Reply
</oj-button>

<oj-button
        class="oj-flex-item oj-sm-padding-1x-end"
        on-oj-action='[[escalatePriority]]'
        disabled="[[priority() === 1]]">
        <span slot='startIcon' class='fas fa-hand-point-up'></span>
        Escalate Priority
</oj-button>

<oj-button
        class="oj-flex-item oj-sm-padding-1x-end"
        on-oj-action='[[confirmCloseDialog]]'>
        <span slot='startIcon' class='fas fa-times-circle'></span>
        Close Ticket
</oj-button>
```

Ticket Closure Dialog

Before a user is able to close a ticket, he or she must first confirm the closure and provide a reason for closing the ticket. For this, an Oracle JET Dialog component will be opened as soon as the user clicks the Close Ticket button.

Add ojs/ojselectcombobox, ojs/ojlabel, and ojs/ojdialog to the define block within view-ticket.js and then add Listing 9-5 to the end of the view-ticket.html file.

Listing 9-5. Closure Confirmation Dialog

```
<oj-dialog style="display:none" id="close-confirmation-dialog"
title="Confirm Closure">
    <div slot="body">
        Are you sure you wish to close this ticket?

        <oj-label for="closure-reason" class="oj-sm-padding-4x-top">
        Reason for closure</oj-label>
        <oj-select-one id="closure-reason" value="{{closureReason}}">
            <oj-option value="Ticket Answered">Ticket answered
            </oj-option>
            <oj-option value="Workaround Provided">Workaround
            Provided</oj-option>
            <oj-option value="No longer an issue">No longer an
            issue</oj-option>
            <oj-option value="Other">Other</oj-option>
        </oj-select-one>
    </div>
    <div slot="footer">
        <oj-button id="cancel-close" on-oj-action="[[closeDialog]]">Cancel
        </oj-button>
        <oj-button id="confirm-close" class='oj-button-confirm'
        on-oj-action="[[closeTicket]]">Close
        </oj-button>
    </div>
</oj-dialog>
```

Within the dialog, a Select One Choice component is used for the reason drop-down list, as well as a button component to confirm or cancel the closure.

Signal Listeners

Next, we will add the listeners to the `ticket-desk.js` file. Both listener functions will implement the `save` method that comes with the ojModel class. The `save` method will call the API end point with the `PUT HTTP` method. The first parameter into the `save` method should be the attributes to be changed, followed by a second parameter of options. The options parameter may include the following:

- `Success`: Callback when the save has been successful.

- `Error`: Callback when the save has failed.

- `contentType`: Change the content type to something other than the default (application/json).

- `validate`: Specifies whether validation should be run

- `wait`: Wait for a success before updating the model.

- `patch`: Change the call to be a PATCH.

- `attrs`: Pass attributes to control those that are saved to the server.

Add the `updatePrioritySignal` listener from Listing 9-6. The `ticketId` parameter (which is passed into the signals by the dispatch event) will contain the ticket ID and will be used to form the `updatedData` object. The new `updatedData` object is used when calling the `save` method.

Listing 9-6. `updatePrioritySignal`

```
/* Priority update listener, when a dispatch signal is sent, the priority
is increased and the model item updated */

self.updatePrioritySignal.add(function(ticketId) {
        var newPriority;
        var modelItem = self.ticketList().get(ticketId);
        var modelData = modelItem.attributes;

        newPriority = modelData.priority - 1;

        var updatedData = {
          id: modelData.id,
          priority: newPriority
        };
```

```
      modelItem.save(updatedData, {
        wait: true,
        success: function (model, response, options) {
          console.log('Success');
          self.selectedTicketModel(self.ticketList().get(self.
          selectedTicket()[0]))
        },
        error: function (jqXHR) {
          console.log('Error');
        }
      });
});
```

The next signal listener to add is for closeTicketSignal. This signal will accept two parameters, both ticketId and closureReason. Add Listing 9-7 into ticket-desk.js.

Listing 9-7. closeTicketSignal

```
/* Close ticket listener, when a dispatch signal is sent, the new object
with closed status is created and the model item is updated */

self.closeTicketSignal.add(function(ticketId, closureReason) {
      var modelItem = self.ticketList().get(ticketId);

      var modelData = modelItem.attributes;

      var updatedData = {
        id: modelData.id,
        status: 'Closed',
   closureReason: closureReason
      };

      modelItem.save(updatedData, {
       wait:true,
        success: function (model, response, options) {
          console.log('Success');
          self.selectedTicketModel(self.ticketList().get(self.
          selectedTicket()[0]))
        },
```

```
      error: function (jqXHR) {
        console.log('Error');
      }
    });
})
```

Figure 9-2 illustrates the new buttons with FontAwesome icons, as well as a disabled Escalate Priority button, as the priority is at 1 and cannot go any higher.

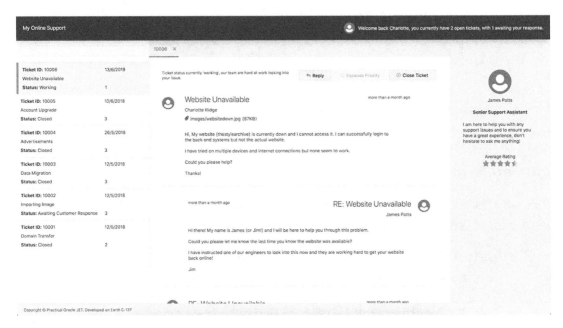

Figure 9-2. *Ticket Management buttons with icons and disabled Escalate Priority*

Adding Ticket Ratings

When a ticket has been closed, we should hide the ticket management buttons and give the user the option to rate his/her experience. The `ojRatingGauge` component will be used for the rating functionality, so be sure to add `ojs/ojgauge` to the `define` block of `view-ticket.js`.

First, hide the three ticket management buttons in `view-ticket.html` by wrapping them in an `ojBindIf` component, so that the buttons only show if the ticket is not closed.

```
<oj-bind-if test="[[status() != 'Closed']]">
</oj-bind-if>
```

Then again, using ojBindIf, check if a ticket is closed and render the ojRatingGauge component. The component will use the closedTicketRatingValue variable as its value. If the value is -1, the ticket has not yet been rated, and the component is taken out of read-only mode.

If the component is not in read-only mode, a user is able to select a star to specify a rating. Selecting a star will fire a value change event, and the attribute on-value-change binds to the ratingValueChanged function that sets the rating value.

```
<oj-bind-if test="[[status() == 'Closed']]">
    <div class="oj-sm-6 oj-flex oj-sm-justify-content-flex-end">
        <oj-rating-gauge
            id="closed-ticket-rating"
            class="oj-sm-6 oj-flex-item"
            value="{{closedTicketRatingValue}}"
            on-value-changed="[[ratingValueChanged]]"
            selected-state.color="#E74C3C"
            readonly="[[closedTicketRatingValue() > 0]]"
            style="height:30px;">
        </oj-rating-gauge>
    </div>
</oj-bind-if>
```

Within the ViewModel, add the new variable and the event listener:

```
self.closedTicketRatingValue = ko.observable();

self.ratingValueChanged = function(event) {
    self.closedTicketRatingValue(event.detail['value']);
}
```

Ensure that the closedTicketRatingValue variable is populated with a value returned from the API, by adding the following into the computed ticketModel function:

```
self.closedTicketRatingValue(params.ticketModel().get('ticketRating'));
```

Finally, when a ticket is closed, we should disable the Reply button at the bottom of a ticket. To do this, set the disabled attribute on the Reply button, so that it looks like the following:

```
<oj-button id='reply-button' on-oj-action='[[ticketReply]]'
    disabled="[[status() === 'Closed']]">
    <span slot='startIcon' class='fas fa-reply'></span>
    Reply
</oj-button>
```

Now when running the application and clicking the close button for ticket 10006, you should be presented with the confirmation dialog similar to that in Figure 9-3.

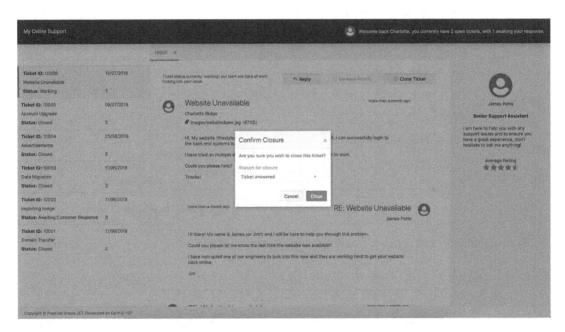

Figure 9-3. *Ticket closure confirmation*

After clicking Close on the confirmation, the ticket should have a status of closed, and you are able to rate the ticket using the rating gauge, as shown in Figure 9-4.

Figure 9-4. *Closed ticket with a five-star rating*

Summary

With the completion of this chapter, you have used the Signals library that comes bundled with an Oracle JET application. Two new signals have been created, one for closing a ticket and one for updating the ticket priority. Both signals communicate with the parent module (ticket desk) that uses the ojModel save method to submit the changes to the service. The save method updates the model locally, meaning we can see the updated application state instantly.

You also have used an Oracle JET Dialog and Select One Choice component for creating a closure confirmation step.

Finally, you have used the Oracle JET Rating Gauge visualization again, this time for providing the ability to rate tickets after they have been closed.

CHAPTER 10

Search Component

In this chapter, we are going to explore the Oracle JET Custom Web Component Architecture and use it to build a search component. The component will automatically filter down the ticket list as the user is typing, to instantly show the results and reduce the amount of actions required by the user. This aspect of showing results while the user types will be achieved easily, thanks to the component's writeback properties facilitating the communication between the component and the consuming ViewModel.

The topic of JET Web Components is quite extensive, and within the use case that follows, I will be covering only some of the features that the architecture provides. I recommend that you spend time reviewing the JET Web Components documentation, to really understand the full architecture.

Why Components?

As a developer, you should already be familiar with the concept of components. They are a defined set of properties, methods, and events associated with a piece of code. Components offer the benefit of reusability (both within the same application or across multiple applications), encapsulation, and easy-to-consume functionality. To achieve all this, a certain set of standards must be in place. Web Components in Oracle JET follows the standards set out within the W3C Web Component Specification.

As web applications have become more complex, the amount of markup and backing logic has too. Increasing amounts of markup and logic result in pages that are crowded with various widgets that cannot be easily reused in different areas of an application. Take a carousel as an example. A carousel is a common web site feature and could have the following markup:

```
<div id='main-carousel'>
    <!-- Carousel Panels -->
    <div class='carousel-panel'>
```

© Daniel Curtis 2019
D. Curtis, *Practical Oracle JET*, https://doi.org/10.1007/978-1-4842-4346-6_10

```
            <img src='jupiter.jpg' alt='Jupiter' />
            <span>Jupiter</span>
    </div>
    <div class='carousel-panel'>
            <img src='mars.jpg' alt='Mars' />
            <span>Mars</span>
    </div>
    <div class='carousel-panel'>
            <img src='saturn.jpg' alt='Saturn' />
            <span>Saturn</span>
    </div>

    <!-- Controls -->
    <a href='#' class='left-arrow'></a>
    <a href='#' class='right-arrow'></a>
</div>
```

Now imagine all this markup packaged into a simple Web Component.

```
<main-carousel panels="[[panels]]"></main-carousel>
```

The carousel is just one example, and often, web applications have multiple different widgets, combined to achieve the complete functionality. It is clear to see that moving widgets into separate components is a good idea for cleaning up the markup of a page, but Web Components offer more than that, they make available events, full API definition, and much more.

Note   If you come from an ADF background, you may be familiar with the ADF flavor of components: *declarative components*. In Oracle JET, we have *Web Components*.

Creating Your First Component

Creating a JET component for the first time is relatively straightforward. The Oracle JET tooling will do all the hard work for you. The tooling will scaffold all the files you need to get started. Run the following command in the UI directory:

```
ojet create component inline-search
```

Note   It is best practice to apply a namespace to your components, to avoid any naming collisions. All Oracle JET components are prefixed with the namespace oj-.

Once that command has finished, you should now see a new jet-composites directory appear within the js folder, with your newly created component inside. See Figure 10-1 for what that result looks like.

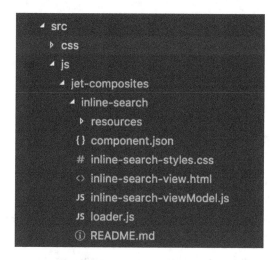

Figure 10-1. *New Oracle JET Web Component*

Figure 10-1 shows a number of files. Let's take a look at what the roles of each of these files are. The following subsections offer a little bit of detail about each one.

loader.js

Figure 10-2 shows the contents of the loader.js file. Think of this file as the entry point into the component. It loads all the libraries required to register the component (View, ViewModel, and metadata), so that the component can be initialized later within your consuming module. We will be including this file into the ticket desk ViewModel shortly.

```
/**
  Copyright (c) 2015, 2018, Oracle and/or its affiliates.
  The Universal Permissive License (UPL), Version 1.0
*/
define(['ojs/ojcomposite',
        'text!./inline-search-view.html',
        './inline-search-viewModel',
        'text!./component.json',
        'css!./inline-search-styles'],
  function(Composite, view, viewModel, metadata) {
    Composite.register('inline-search', {
      view: view,
      viewModel: viewModel,
      metadata: JSON.parse(metadata)
    });
  }
);
```

Figure 10-2. `loader.js` *file*

component.json

Next comes `component.json`. This file is responsible for defining the component
API. The file will define the properties, methods, and events that the component will
support. Also defined in the file are the metadata elements, such as name, version, and
description.

There will be some automatically generated content in the file. Replace that default
content with the following:

```
{
  "name": "inline-search",
  "displayName": "inline-search",
  "description": "A search component for searching through a collection",
  "version": "1.0.0",
  "jetVersion": "^6.0.0",
  "properties": {
    "data": {
      "description": "Collection passed into the component that can be
      filtered down.",
      "type": "oj.Collection",
      "writeback": true
    },
```

```
    "models": {
      "description": "An array of models passed to the component used to
      reset the collection.",
      "type": "Array"
    },
    "filterAttribute": {
      "description": "The attribute that the search string will be matched
      against.",
      "type": "string"
    }
  },
  "methods" : {
    "resetSearch" : {
      "description" : "A function to clear the search value",
      "internalName" : "_resetSearch"
    }
  }
}
```

Now we have set the name of the component, its description, and versioning information. Also included are three properties:

- data: This is the collection object that is used for the ticket list. The collection will be filtered down if a user specifies a search term, and the new collection will be written back to the consuming module.

- models: This is a list of the persisting models. This list will never change during a search and will be used to reset the collection to its original state, once a search term is removed.

- filterAttribute: The attribute that the search term will match against

There are several notable extra options that you can set on component properties. These are

- description: A description for the property

- type: The type of the property: string, number, Boolean, array, or object

- `value`: Default value for the property

- `readOnly`: Boolean value to determine if a property can be updated outside of the ViewModel

- `writeback`: Boolean value to determine whether any variables bound to the property could be written back to

- `enumValues`: An array of valid enumeration values used for when the property type is string. An error is thrown if a property value is mismatched with this list.

A method has been defined within the `components.json` file. Methods are a way of creating functions within the component that can be accessible outside the component during runtime.

Built-in Events

All properties for Web Components come with "built-in" events. These events are triggered whenever a property's value changes and are known as *property changed events*. There are two ways to hook onto property changed events: within the component itself or within the consuming ViewModel.

From within the component, you can create an event listener, using the naming standard of `dataChanged` (appending `Changed` to the end of the property name).

From within the consuming module, the attribute `on-data-changed` can be added to the component element, to handle the event listening from the consuming side. We will be using the `on-data-changed` attribute shortly.

Events and Slots

There are two other attributes (in addition to properties and methods) that you can define within `components.json`. They are not used for this example, but here is a quick overview of what they are:

- `events`: As well as the built-in events mentioned, it is also possible to create custom events. You have full control over when these events are raised and can define exactly what detail values are passed as part of the event.

- slots: We have already explored the concept of slots when adding an icon to a button. To recap, a slot is a predefined area within a component in which you can "slot" in your own markup. It is possible to create custom slot areas within a Web Component.

inline-search-viewModel.js

The bulk of the component logic will go within the inline-search-viewModel.js file. Upon opening the file, your first task is to change the name of the function from ExampleComponentModel to InlineSearchModel, and ensure that you update the return statement to reflect this change.

Now replace the sample observable 'messageText' with the following variables:

```
// Variable Setup
self.collectionToBeFiltered = ko.observable(context.properties.data);
self.persistentModels = [];
self.filterAttribute = ko.observable(context.properties.filterAttribute);
self.searchTerm = ko.observable();
```

When the component is initialized, we want to populate the collectionToBeFiltered and filterAttribute variables with the properties that we will be passing into the component. These can be accessed using the context object that is passed into the InlineSearchModel function.

The other variable that must be populated is the persistentModels array. The array will be populated after the fact, because as you will see shortly, the models are loaded in after the collection has resolved on the consuming ViewModel, meaning they are not available upon initialization of the component. To access this property, we must use a life cycle event available on Web Components. Add the propertyChanged life cycle event into the ViewModel, and it will be automatically triggered when the models are assigned.

```
/* Wait for models to be passed in and when they are assign them to the
persistentModels variable */
self.propertyChanged = function(event){
    if(event.property === 'models'){
        self.persistentModels = event.value;
    }
}
```

Now we must implement the search logic, which will be carried out by two functions. The first of the two functions is `valueFilter`, which is responsible for checking if the entered value matches with one of the models. The `valueFilter` function is invoked by a comparator when searching through the collection. Insert the following code into the `inline-search-viewModel.js` file:

```
/* Filter for checking if the entered values matches with one of the model
attributes */
self.valueFilter = function (model, attr, value) {
            var name = model.get(attr);
            return (name.toLowerCase().indexOf(value.toLowerCase()) > -1);
};
```

The second of the two functions will be placed within a `subscribe` method on the `searchTerm` observable. The `subscribe` method in Knockout will listen on an observable and notify the callback function of any changes anytime a user types into the search box.

The callback function is responsible for the following:

- Checking whether the length of the term is zero (ie, there is no search term), closing the collection and resetting the clone to its original state using the `persistentModels` variable. The reset method on a collection accepts an array of models and resets the collection object to this new array of models. The cloned collection will then be passed back into the data property, and because the data property has the `'writeback'` attribute set, the changed data will be written back to the consuming ViewModel.

- Checking whether the length of the term is more than zero. If so, the function will create an object using the `filteredAttribute` value that we populated earlier, then the where method will be used on the collection to find matching model objects. The collection will be cloned and the cloned collection will be reset with the new filtered models. The clone will be passed back to the consuming ViewModel.

Add the following code below the valueFilter function created earlier:

```
/* Function to handle the filtering of the collection when a user enters a
value into the search box */
self.searchTerm.subscribe(function (newValue) {
  if (newValue.length == 0) {
    var clonedCollection = self.collectionToBeFiltered().clone()
    clonedCollection.reset(self.persistentModels);
    context.properties.data = clonedCollection
  } else {
    self.collectionToBeFiltered().reset(self.persistentModels);
    var filterObject = {}
    filterObject[self.filterAttribute()] = { value: newValue, comparator:
    self.valueFilter };
    var ret = self.collectionToBeFiltered().where(filterObject);
    var clonedCollection = self.collectionToBeFiltered().clone()
    clonedCollection.reset(ret);
    context.properties.data = clonedCollection
  }
});
```

We now want to use the Knockout extend method to set a rate limit. A rate limit
is used to delay the Knockout observable propagation (and, therefore, the subscribe
notification) by a set period of time. This will prevent the search code from running too
many times when a user types quickly. To set a rate limit, add the following line below
the variable declaration for searchTerm:

```
self.searchTerm.extend({ rateLimit: 500 });
```

resetSearch method

Within the API, we defined the method resetSearch, which will be used to reset the
search box and remove the search term when a user navigates to a ticket that is no longer
present in the ticket list. To implement, add the following code in the components
ViewModel, but outside the InlineSearchModel function:

```
InlineSearchModel.prototype._resetSearch = function () {
    this.searchTerm('')
};
```

To use the method, you simply have to hook onto the component and call the resetSearch method, as defined within the components.json API. Replace the tabSelectionChanged function within ticket-desk.js with the following:

```
self.tabSelectionChanged = function () {
  if(self.ticketList().get(self.selectedTabItem()) === undefined){
      document.getElementById("search-component").resetSearch();
  }

  oj.Context.getContext(document.getElementById("search-component"))
  .getBusyContext()
  .whenReady()
  .then(function () {
      self.selectedTicketModel(self.ticketList().get(self.selectedTabItem()))
      self.selectedTicket([self.selectedTabItem()])
  })
}
```

The conditional statement will check if the selected tab item exists within the ticketList collection, and if it doesn't, reset the ticket list.

You also need to update the conditional check that surrounds the logic within the deleteTab function. Replace the first line to the following:

```
if(id != self.persistentModels()[0].get('id')){
```

inline-search-view.html

Open the inline-search-view.html file. This file holds all the View markup for the component. In our case, it will be a relatively straightforward file that contains an Oracle JET Input Text Component bound to the searchTerm variable.

Note   It is possible to access the component properties directly in the View, if needed. For example, if you wanted to access the data property, you can do so by using the props object ($props.data).

Replace the contents of the View with the following Input Text Component:

```
<oj-input-text
    class="oj-sm-12 oj-sm-padding-3x-vertical oj-sm-padding-2x-horizontal"
    value="{{searchTerm}}"
    raw-value="{{searchTerm}}"
    autocomplete="off">
</oj-input-text>
```

Both the `value` and `raw-value` attributes are being used here. The `raw-value` attribute will update as a user types, whereas the `value` attribute is only updated when the focus is moved away from the component.

Note that the `autocomplete` attribute has been added. This attribute gets passed directly to the HTML input element, to prevent the browser from trying to automatically suggest or complete a user's input.

inline-search-styles.css

Use the `inline-search-styles.css` file to add any custom styling related to the component. As we are not styling the search box at all (other than using the predefined flex classes on the component), no changes are needed on this file.

Consuming the New Component

Now that the new component has been created, it is time to consume the component within the `ticket-desk.js` ViewModel. First, include the new component in the RequireJS config block in the `main.js` file, by adding the following line:

```
'inline-search': 'jet-composites/inline-search/1.0.0'
```

Then include the new component within the `ticket-desk.js` define block:

```
'inline-search/loader'
```

Next, add the following new variables into `ticket-desk.js`. One will hold `persistentModels` once they have been extracted from the collection; the second will hold the attribute that will be used to match the search against. Finally the selectionRequired variable is needed to help us out with a workaround for a bug in the list component, more on this shortly.

```
self.persistentModels = ko.observableArray();
self.filterAttribute = 'title';
self.selectionRequired = ko.observable(true);
```

Then extract the models from the collection, using the fetch method, as shown in the following snippet of code. This is required, as it is not possible to populate persistentModels until after the collection has called the data service. Therefore, we must use the success callback to assign the model values.

```
self.ticketList().fetch({
    success: function success(data) {
        self.persistentModels(data.models);
    }
});
```

Add the following function into the ViewModel. The function will be called when the data property is changed from within the search component, and will update the datasource with the updated collection containing the filtered models. Normally we would not need to do this, but unfortunately at time of writing there is a bug in the Oracle JET ListView component that means we must disable the selection-required attribute and then reassign the datasource again. The alternative if the bug was not present would be to just perform the reset directly on the collection within the search component (without doing the clone), and then allowing the write back functionality take care of updating the ListView for us. The bug should be fixed as part of JET version 6.2.

```
self.updateDataSource = function(event){
    self.selectionRequired(false);
    self.ticketListDataSource(new oj.CollectionTableDataSource(self.
    ticketList()));
    var busyContext = oj.Context.getPageContext().getBusyContext();

    busyContext.whenReady().then(function () {
      self.selectionRequired(true);
    });
}
```

You will also need to update the `'selection-required'` attribute on the list view within `ticket-desk.html`, so that it references the `'selectionRequired'` variable. Finally, replace the temporary input text component within `ticket-desk.html` with the newly created component. Here is how you should define the component:

```
<!-- Search functionality -->
<inline-search
  id="search-component"
    data="{{ticketList}}"
    on-data-changed="[[updateDataSource]]"
    models="[[persistentModels]]"
    filter-attribute='[[filterAttribute]]'>
</inline-search>
<!-- Search functionality -->
```

Note   The kebab case attribute for naming components, `filter-attribute`, will translate to camel case, `filterAttribute`, within the component properties. This is because HTML markup is not case-sensitive, whereas the property names are.

Now, if you re-serve the application, you will be able to use the search functionality to search through all the tickets within the list instantly. Figure 10-3 provides an example, showing a ticket about a web site being unavailable.

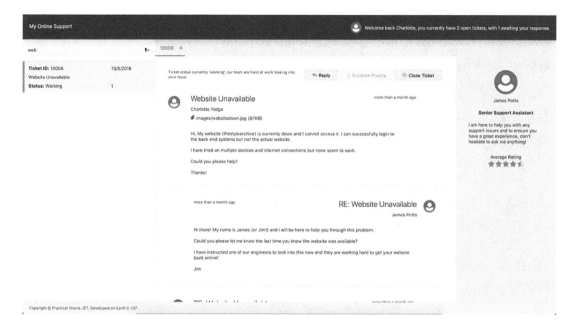

Figure 10-3. *Search functionality using a Web Component*

Summary

In this chapter, you have created your first component and implemented the search functionality, so that it is possible to search through the ticket list. You have done this using Oracle JET Custom Web Components and have learned what features make up this architecture.

Oracle JET Custom Web Components is a crucial part of JET development and should always be at the forefront of your mind. Where possible, you should be considering using Web Components.

CHAPTER 11

Ticket Creation

This chapter covers the functionality to create new tickets, using several Oracle JET components that we have already used (plus some new ones). The Oracle JET Common Model will be used to create new tickets, and we will be using Signals once again to handle the intermodular communication.

Animations will be introduced to alter the way that elements are loaded into a page, which can enrich a user's experience.

The components/libraries used within this chapter are

- *ojBindIf*

- *ojInputText*

- *ojSelectOne*

- *ojModule*

- *AnimationUtils*

- *ojFilePicker*

- *ojButton*

- *ojLabel*

- *FontAwesome*

API Setup

For this chapter, we must create new mock API end points. These end points will be responsible for the creation of new tickets and returning replies for any new tickets created. To that end, create the files shown in Listings 11-1 through 11-3.

© Daniel Curtis 2019
D. Curtis, *Practical Oracle JET*, https://doi.org/10.1007/978-1-4842-4346-6_11

Listing 11-1. API/mocks/tickets/replies/__/GET.mock

```
HTTP/1.1 200 OK
Content-Type: application/json; charset=utf-8
Access-Control-Allow-Origin: *

{
    "notes": []
}
```

Listing 11-2. API/mocks/tickets/POST.mock

```
HTTP/1.1 200 OK
Content-Type: application/json; charset=utf-8
Access-Control-Allow-Origin: *
Access-Control-Allow-Headers: Origin, X-Requested-With, Content-Type, Accept
Access-Control-Allow-Methods: GET, POST, PUT

{}
```

Listing 11-3. API/mocks/tickets/OPTIONS.mock

```
HTTP/1.1 200 OK
Content-Type: application/json; charset=utf-8
Access-Control-Allow-Origin: *
Access-Control-Allow-Headers: Origin, X-Requested-With, Content-Type, Accept
```

Create a Ticket Module

Throughout the chapter, we will be working on a new module that will hold all
the markup and logic for creating a new ticket. Add two files to define the module:
viewModels/create-ticket.js and views/create-ticket.html. Within the view,
include some placeholder text, such as "This is the create ticket module!"

The new module definition should be included within the ticket-desk.html
file, between the tab bar section and the selected ticket section. This module will not
always be visible, so it should be wrapped within an ojBindIf component, as shown in
Listing 11-4.

Listing 11-4. Create New Ticket Module

```
<!-- Create New Ticket Module -->
<oj-bind-if test="[[createVisible]]">
    <div data-bind="ojModule: { name: 'create-ticket',
    params: {createNewTicketSignal: createNewTicketSignal,
                    newTicketId: newTicketId}
    }">
    </div>
</oj-bind-if>
<!-- Create New Ticket Module -->
```

The visibility of the new module will be controlled by a button, which should be included at the end of the tab bar container (there should be three columns available at the end of the tab bar for the button to occupy). Add Listing 11-5 just before the closing div for the tab bar container, within the `ticket-desk.html` file.

Listing 11-5. Create New Ticket Button

```
<div class="oj-flex oj-sm-3 oj-sm-justify-content-flex-end oj-sm-padding-4x-end">
      <oj-bind-if test="[[!createVisible()]]">
        <oj-button on-oj-action="[[toggleCreateTicket]]">
          <span slot="startIcon" class='fas fa-plus'></span>
          Create New Ticket
        </oj-button>
      </oj-bind-if>
      <oj-bind-if test="[[createVisible]]">
        <oj-button on-oj-action="[[toggleCreateTicket]]">
          <span slot="startIcon" class='fas fa-ban'></span>
          Cancel
        </oj-button>
      </oj-bind-if>
</div>
```

Within `ticket-desk.js`, add the following two variables:

```
self.createVisible = ko.observable(false)
self.newTicketId = '';
```

The createVisible variable is responsible for holding the visible state of the create ticket module, and newTicketId will hold the unique identifier for new tickets. I will address why holding the unique identifier is needed, shortly.

A new signal is also required, and this signal will be responsible for notifying the ticket desk module when a new ticket must be added to the ticket list collection. Include the following in the variables section:

```
self.createNewTicketSignal = new signals.Signal();
```

Create a new function named toggleCreateTicket to handle the showing and hiding of the module. For now, this will only show the module, and we will build on the functionality later in the chapter. Create the function using the following code as its definition:

```
/*
    Toggle the state of the create ticket module
*/
self.toggleCreateTicket = function () {
        self.createVisible(true)
}
```

By running the application, you should now see the create ticket button at the top right of the tab bar, as shown in Figure 11-1. Clicking the button will cause the button to change state and the create ticket module to appear directly above the ticket content.

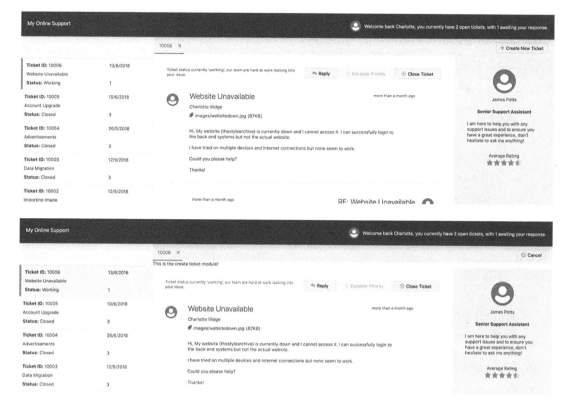

Figure 11-1. *Show/hide create ticket module*

Adding Animation

Animation can be great for improving user experience when used correctly in enterprise applications. By using animation, you can create a sense of transition between tasks and give the user a little perspective on the way that the application is structured and navigated through.

Instead of just having the ticket creation module appear, we are going to implement a sliding-down animation, to give the effect of the module sliding and pushing the rest of the content farther down the page. A user is then aware that the rest of the ticket content is still visible farther down the page, if he/she wants to scroll down and access it.

Oracle JET comes with a built-in library for handling animations. It provides the ability to hook onto elements and configure various different animation options. To include an animation for the create ticket module, we are going to take advantage of the life cycle listeners that were explored in Chapter 8.

Open the create ticket ViewModel file and create the standard `define` block and `ViewModel` function, as shown following:

```
define(['ojs/ojcore',
    'knockout',
    'jquery'
],
    function (oj, ko, $) {
        function CreateTicketViewModel (params) {
        var self = this;
        }
        return CreateTicketViewModel;
    }
);
```

Update the `create-ticket` view to wrap the existing placeholder in a div with the ID of `create-new-ticket`, so that the `create-ticket.html` file looks like the following:

```
<div id="create-new-ticket" class="oj-sm-padding-4x">
    This is the create ticket module!
</div>
```

In Chapter 8, I discussed life cycle events. Next, we are going to be using the `handleAttached` life cycle method, which is executed when the module has been attached to the DOM. Within the `handleAttached` function, we will call the `animationsUtils` method, to initialize the animation on the `create-new-ticket` element. Here's the code to include within `create-ticket.js`:

```
self.handleAttached = function () {
    oj.AnimationUtils['slideIn']($('#create-new-ticket')[0], {
'direction': 'bottom' });
}
```

There are several different animations available, including fade, flip, slide, zoom, expand/collapse, and ripple. There are two parameters that can be passed into `animationUtils`, the first is the element that will be animated, and the second is an options object. The `options` parameter accepts an object of different configurations to apply to the animation. The options vary with the different animation types, but some common ones are delay, duration, and direction. In the preceding example, the direction property is being set.

The sliding-in animation is now taken care of. However, the sliding-out animation will have to be implemented differently, as it must be executed before the module is closed. The animation should be run from within the `ticket-desk.js` file instead of using the `handleAttached` event within create-ticket.js. Open the file and replace the contents of the `toggleCreateTicket` function with the following:

```
if (self.createVisible() === true) {
    oj.AnimationUtils['slideOut']($('#create-new-ticket')[0], {
    'direction': 'top' }).then(function () {
      self.createVisible(false);
    });
  }
  else {
    self.createVisible(true);
}
```

Now, when clicking the button, you should see the module animate when opening and closing. Unfortunately, it is not possible to include a GIF in this book, to show this in action. Maybe one day!

Building the Creation Form

It is time to build the functionality and create the form to capture new ticket details. This will include the ticket title, priority, and summary of the issue. The form will be made up of ojLabel components for specifying field labels, an ojInputText component for the ticket title, an ojSelectOne component for the priority selection, and, finally, the `trumbowyg` editor.

An ojSelectOne component provides the functionality for a LOV (list of values) selection. The component can have a list of options attached to it that a user is able to select. These options can either be hard-coded into the markup (as we will be doing shortly), or they can be dynamically data-driven from the ViewModel. The component comes with a bunch of other features too, such as the ability to group options, add images to options, and it even provides the functionality to search through the available options.

Include the following code in Listing 11-6 inside the create-new-ticket element in the create-ticket View:

Listing 11-6. Create New Ticket Form

```
<div class="oj-sm-padding-4x">
        <h2>Create a new ticket</h2>
        <oj-label for="title" class="oj-sm-padding-2x-top">Title:</oj-label>
        <oj-input-text id="title" value="{{newTicketTitle}}"></oj-input-text>
        <oj-label for="pirority" class="oj-sm-padding-2x-top">Priority:
        </oj-label>
        <oj-select-one id="pirority" value="{{newTicketPriority}}">
            <oj-option value="1">1 - Blocker</oj-option>
            <oj-option value="2">2 - Critical</oj-option>
            <oj-option value="3">3 - High</oj-option>
            <oj-option value="4">4 - Medium</oj-option>
            <oj-option value="5">5 - Low</oj-option>
        </oj-select-one>
            <oj-label for="new-ticket-area" class="oj-sm-padding-2x-
            top">Issue Summary:</oj-label>
        <div id="new-ticket-area"></div>
</div>
```

Note   The for attribute on the ojLabel component should match the ID of the element that the label corresponds to.

Within the create-ticket.js file, add ojs/ojselectcombobox and trumbowyg in the define block, then add the following two variables:

```
self.newTicketTitle = ko.observable();
self.newTicketPriority = ko.observable();
```

Within the handleAttached function, add the initialization for the editor, with the same configuration that was used for the ticket replies, as follows:

```
$('#new-ticket-area').trumbowyg(
                 {
                      btns: ['bold', 'italic', 'underline'],
                      resetCss: true,
                      removeformatPasted: true
                 }
);
```

Create a new CSS class in the containers SASS partial (base/containers.scss), to set the background color on the create-new-ticket element.

```
#create-new-ticket {
    background-color: $neutral-color;
}
```

When opening the create ticket module, the form should look similar to that in Figure 11-2.

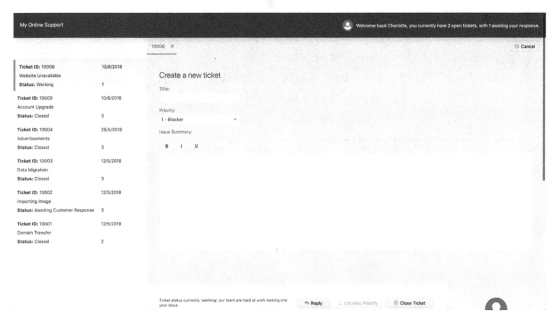

Figure 11-2. *Create New Ticket Form*

Adding Attachments and Form Submission

In the same way that an attachment can be added to ticket replies, new tickets creation will allow for attachment uploading. Therefore, we will be doing some refactoring, to make the file upload code reusable across both creation and replies.

First, include Listing 11-7 within the create-ticket View, under the new-ticket-area element. Other than label updates, this remains unchanged from the reply ticket markup.

Listing 11-7. File Attachments and Form Submission

```
<div class="oj-flex-bar oj-sm-padding-2x-top">
        <div class="oj-flex-bar-start oj-sm-align-items-center">
            <oj-file-picker class='oj-filepicker-custom oj-sm-padding-
            2x-end' id="fileUpload" selectOn='click'
                on-oj-select='[[fileSelectionListener]]'
                accept="[[allowedFileTypes]]" selection-mode='single'>
                <oj-button slot='trigger'>
                    <span slot='startIcon' class='fas fa-upload'></span>
                    File Upload
                </oj-button>
            </oj-file-picker>
            <oj-bind-if test='[[uploadedFile()[0]]]'>
                <oj-bind-text value="[[uploadedFile()[0].name]]">
                </oj-bind-text>
            </oj-bind-if>
        </div>
        <div class="oj-flex-bar-end">
            <oj-bind-if test="[[createInProgress() === false]]">
                <oj-button id='reply-button' on-oj-action='[[createTicket]]'
                class="oj-button-confirm" disabled="[[createInProgress]]">
                    <span slot='startIcon' class="fas fa-reply"></span>
                    Create Ticket
                </oj-button>
            </oj-bind-if>
```

```
<oj-bind-if test="[[createInProgress]]">
    <oj-button id='create-button' class="oj-button-confirm"
    disabled="true">
        <span slot='startIcon' class="fas fa-circle-notch
        fa-spin"></span>
        Creating Ticket
    </oj-button>
</oj-bind-if>
    </div>
</div>
```

Before building the ViewModel, we are going to create some reusable functions within the appUtils file. The purpose of Listing 11-8 is the same as when it was implemented on the ticket replies; however, there are a couple of differences in how we achieve that end goal.

The first is how the function returns the result to the consuming ViewModel. A promise is used here because we are dealing with an anyscronous request and we need to wait for a response before assigning the value.

Second, we are passing in ticketId from the ticket-desk.js file. At the time of creating a new ticket there will not yet be an ID, and the upload API requires a ticket ID to know which ticket the upload relates to. Assuming the ticket ID value is always incremented by 1, we can take the latest ticketId value and increment it by 1, and the back end can handle linking the ticket and attachment and clearing out attachments that do not link to a ticket.

Finally, return the attachment object back to the consuming ViewModel, so that it can be appended to the ticket request. To implement, open the appUtils.js file and include the new uploadAttachment function (Listing 11-8).

Listing 11-8. uploadAttachment Function

```
/* Function to upload the new attachment and return a promise */
        self.uploadAttachment = function (ticketId, uploadedFile) {
          var date = new Date();
          var attachment = [];
```

```
                return new Promise(
                    function (resolve, reject) {
                        var file = $("#fileUpload").find("input")[0].files[0];
                        var data = new FormData();
                        data.append("file", file);
                        $.ajax({
                            type: "POST",
                            url: "http://localhost:8080/tickets/upload/" +
                            ticketId,
                            contentType: false,
                            processData: false,
                            data: data,
                            success: function (result) {
                                attachment = [{
                                    "filePath": uploadedFile.name,
                                    "fileSize": self.bytesToSize
                                    (uploadedFile.size),
                                    "timestamp": date.toISOString()
                                }]
                                resolve(attachment)
                            },
                            error: function (err, status, errorThrown) {
                                reject(err);
                                console.error("Error")
                            }
                        });
                    }
                );
    }
```

Add the bytesToSize function created previously into the appUtils file.

```
/*
    Source: http://codeaid.net/javascript/convert-size-in-bytes-to-human-
    readable-format-(javascript)#comment-1
*/
```

```
self.bytesToSize = function (bytes) {
    var sizes = ['Bytes', 'KB', 'MB', 'GB', 'TB'];
    if (bytes == 0) return 'n/a';
            var i = parseInt(Math.floor(Math.log(bytes) / Math.log(1024)));
            return Math.round(bytes / Math.pow(1024, i), 2) + ' '
            + sizes[i];
};
```

Now return to the create new ticket ViewModel and ensure that the appUtils library is included within the define block and passed into the callback function.

Create the following new variables:

```
self.uploadedFile = ko.observableArray([]);
self.allowedFileTypes = ko.observableArray(['image/*']);
self.createNewTicketSignal = params.createNewTicketSignal;
self.newTicketId = params.newTicketId;
self.createInProgress = ko.observable(false);
```

The createTicket function will build a new object (newTicket) and pass it as part of the signal dispatch, so that it can be used to create the new ticket within ticket-desk. js, which we will set up shortly. The function also calls the uploadAttachment utility function if an attachment has been added.

The fileSelectionListener is executed when a user has selected a file to upload and will assign the file details to the uploadedFile variable.

Add Listing 11-9 into create-ticket.js.

Listing 11-9. createTicket Function

```
/* Function to create a new ticket */
self.createTicket = function () {
            var date = new Date();
            var messageArea = $('#new-ticket-area').trumbowyg('html');

            self.createInProgress(true);
            var newTicket = {
                "id": self.newTicketId,
                "title": self.newTicketTitle(),
                "author": "Charlotte Illidge",
```

```
                "representativeId": "1",
                "priority": self.newTicketPriority(),
                "service": "stylearchive",
                "dateCreated": date.toISOString(),
                "status": "New",
                "message": messageArea,
                "attachment": [],
                "ticketRating": -1
        }

        if (self.uploadedFile()[0] != null) {
            appUtils.uploadAttachment(self.newTicketId,
            self.uploadedFile()[0])
                .then(function (attachment) {
                    newTicket['attachment'] = attachment;
                    self.createNewTicketSignal.dispatch(newTicket);
                });
        }
        else {
            self.createNewTicketSignal.dispatch(newTicket);
        }
    }

    self.fileSelectionListener = function (event) {
        var file = event.detail.files
        self.uploadedFile(file)
    }
```

Like ticket replies, the create method on a collection will be used to add the new model onto the ticket list collection. In the following code, the at attribute is passed into the callback, and this adds the new model to index 0 in the collection array. This will ensure that the newest ticket created will be at the top of the ticket list.

Once the new ticket creation has been a success, the listener will then also push the new model to the persistentModels array, so that the new ticket will be searchable, and it will also increment the newTicketId by 1, ready for the next new ticket.

Create the new signal listener by adding the following code into `ticket-desk.js`:

```
/* New ticket creation listener, when a dispatch signal is sent */
self.createNewTicketSignal.add(function (newModel) {
    self.ticketList().create(newModel, {
        wait: true,
        at: 0,
        success: function (model, response, options) {
          self.toggleCreateTicket();
          self.persistentModels.push(model)
          self.newTicketId = self.ticketList().models[0].id + 1;
          console.log('Success')
        },
        error: function (err, status, errorThrown) {
          console.error("Error")
        }
    })
})
```

When the ticket list is initially loaded, the `newTicketId` variable must be set after the collection has been initialized. To do this, add the following line of code within the `fetch` method for the ticket list collection:

```
self.newTicketId = data.models[0].id + 1;
```

Now, when creating a new ticket, you should first see the creation button change to a loading animation, and once the creation has succeeded, the new ticket will be added to the ticket list. Figure 11-3 shows a ticket creation in progress, while Figure 11-4 shows a newly created ticket.

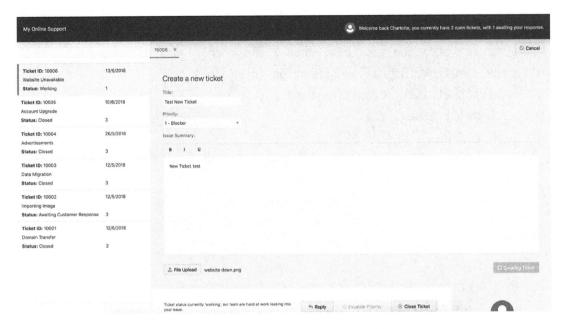

Figure 11-3. *Ticket creation in progress*

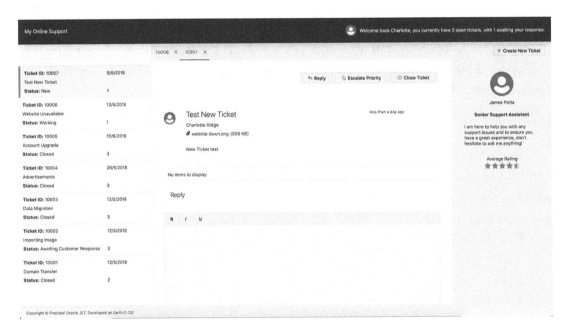

Figure 11-4. *New ticket created*

New Status and Zero Replies

You may notice a couple of issues when viewing a newly created ticket, the first being that there is no status message to the left of the ticket buttons, and the second that there are no replies to the ticket yet, so the message "No items to display" is shown. Let's tidy this up a little.

Within `view-ticket.js`, find the `ticketStatus` function and add the following conditional statement to the end:

```
else if (status === "New") {
                return "This is a new ticket that will be looked into
                shortly by a member of the team. Please check back soon."
}
```

Then change the text that is displayed when there are zero items. To do this, add the following attribute to the list component within `view-ticket.html`:

```
translations.msg-no-data="There are currently no replies to this ticket. If
you need to add extra information please reply to the ticket below."
```

Figure 11-5 illustrates how new tickets should now look, and you can interact with the new ticket in the same way you could with the existing tickets. Try searching, closing, or replying to the new ticket.

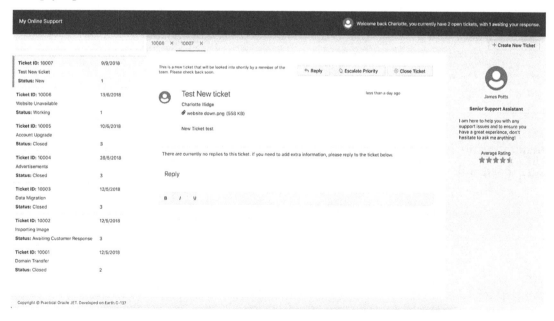

Figure 11-5. *Updated new ticket view*

Refactor Ticket Replies

As the upload functionality is common between create and reply, we must now refactor the reply area to use the common utility function for uploading attachments. Within view-ticket.js remove the uploadFile function, then replace the old promise call within the ticketReply function with the new appUtils upload. The ticketReply function should now look like Listing 11-10.

Listing 11-10. ticketReply Function

```
self.ticketReply = function () {
    var date = new Date();
    var attachment = [];
    if (self.uploadedFile()[0] != null) {
        appUtils.uploadAttachment(self.ticketId(), self.uploadedFile()[0])
            .then(function (attachment) {
                attachment = attachment;
                self.addTicketReplytoCollection(attachment, date);
            })
            .catch(function (error) {
                console.log(error)
            })
    } else {
        self.addTicketReplytoCollection(attachment, date);
    }
}
```

Be sure to remove the bytesToSize function too, as this is no longer required. After refactoring the upload functionality on ticket replies, retest the ticket replies, to make sure that it still works as expected.

Summary

In this chapter, you have set up ticket creation within the application, and to do this, you have used Oracle JET animations, combined with life cycle listeners to hide/show the ticket creation area. As well as this, you have also built upon the skills and components used in previous chapters to upload files and add new models to a collection.

Refactoring existing code is often needed in any type of development, and here you've seen how easy it is to refactor existing code when it is required in multiple places, by moving functions into a common utility file.

CHAPTER 12

Logging, Messages, and Validation

With the core functionality of the application complete, we will now look at three areas that have not yet been explored: logging, messages, and validation. Until now, all log entries have used the built-in browser logging tools, and in this chapter, we will look at how this can be enhanced using components available with the JET toolkit.

Two other areas that have not been considered are messages and validation. We will explore how to provide message feedback to users when they interact with the application and how to use the validation utilities within JET.

The following components will be explored:

- *ojLogger*

- *ojMessages*

- *ojValidation*

- *ojLabel*

- *ojInputText*

Logging

Browser console logging is a way to log messages to the browser console, to aid with the testing and debugging of a web site. Browser logging provides a simple option to see what is happening at certain points within the application.

The standard browser logging is useful when quickly trying to log an output, but as with using `System.out.println` in Java, it shouldn't really be used in production environments, as it can lack the support of features such as global logging levels.

© Daniel Curtis 2019
D. Curtis, *Practical Oracle JET*, https://doi.org/10.1007/978-1-4842-4346-6_12

Oracle JET comes with its own logging component, with different levels of logging. In JET applications, it is advised to use the Oracle JET logger instead of the built-in browser console loggers. The output will still be logged to the console by default.

The logging levels available to use are the following:

- *Error*: Will write an error message to the console

- *Info*: Will write an information message to the console

- *Warn*: Will write a warning message to the console

- *Log*: Will write a general message to the console

To use the JET logging component, you must first set the logging level. To do this, navigate to the appController.js file and set the logging level as "info." For production, you should set the level to "error," to reduce the number of messages cluttering the console. Following is the line of code to add to appController.js:

```
oj.Logger.option("level",  oj.Logger.LEVEL_INFO);
```

Next, find all the occurrences of log messages and replace them with the Oracle JET logger instead. To find all the instances, you can use the built-in search within Visual Studio Code (or your IDE of choice).

For example, within the createNewTicketSignal listener in the ticket-desk ViewModel, there is a console message in both the success and error blocks when creating the new collection item. Replace the console message in the success block with the following:

```
oj.Logger.info('New ticket successfully created: ' + model.id);
```

Then replace the console message in the error block with the following. Ensure that the err parameter is passed into the callback. This will hold the information about the error's cause.

```
oj.Logger.error('Error creating new ticket: ' + err.status + ' ' + err.
statusText);
```

To see an error in action, we can fake an error response from the API. Navigate to and open API/mocks/tickets/POST.mock and change the header response code to "404 Not Found" instead of "200 OK," as follows:

```
HTTP/1.1 404 Not Found
```

With the web console open, try creating a new ticket (press F12). You should see something like the error message in Figure 12-1. Don't forget to change the header response code back to 200 afterward.

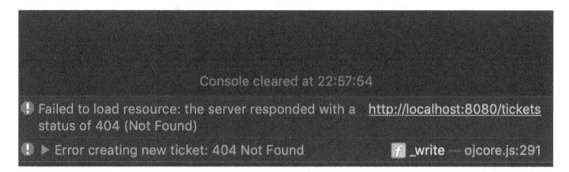

Figure 12-1. *Console error message using ojLogger*

Messages

When a user performs an action within an application, often you will want to provide some sort of feedback to let him or her know whether the action has been successful. Oracle JET has a component available to achieve this: *ojMessages.*

The ojMessages component has a variety of different options to position the messages, change the messages type, and handle properties of the message, such as type and time-outs.

In the following examples, we will be using notification messages positioned at the bottom right-hand corner of the application. There are three actions that we will be specifying events for: ticket closing, escalating priority, and creating a new ticket.

Open ticket-desk.html and include Listing 12-1 at the bottom of the file. It doesn't matter too much where this is positioned in the markup, as the messages will always display in the same position.

Listing 12-1. Message Component Declaration

```
<!-- Start Messages Component -->
    <oj-messages
        id="application-messages"
        messages="{{applicationMessages}}"
```

```
        display="notification"
        position='{
          "my": {"vertical" : "bottom", "horizontal": "end"},
          "at": {"vertical": "bottom", "horizontal": "end"},
          "of": "window"
        }'>
      </oj-messages>
<!-- End Messages Component -->
```

Next, open the `ticket-desk` ViewModel and ensure that `ojs/ojmessages` is included within the `define` block. Then add the following variable, which is responsible for holding any application messages:

```
self.applicationMessages = ko.observableArray([]);
```

Now find the listener for the `createNewTicketSignal`, and in the `success` callback function, add the following:

```
self.applicationMessages.push(
        {
          severity: 'confirmation',
          summary: 'New ticket created',
          detail: 'The new ticket ' + model.id + ' has been created'
        }
)
```

Add the following into the error callback:

```
self.applicationMessages.push(
    {
          severity: 'error',
          summary: 'Error creating ticket',
          detail: 'Error trying to create new ticket'
    }
)
```

By pushing the objects to the `applicationMessages` array, the ojMessages component will automatically display the messages when the service either succeeds or fails. Figure 12-2 shows an example of the ticket creation being successful and the message component showing a success message.

212

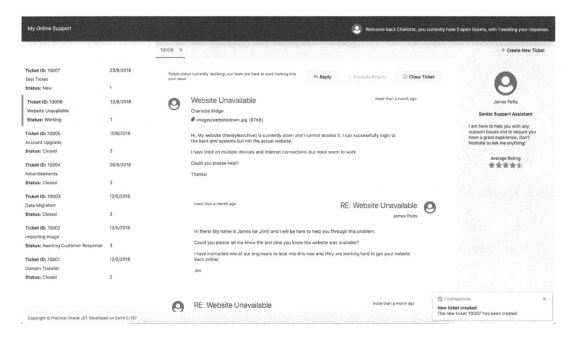

Figure 12-2. *Success message using ojMessages component*

Ticket Priority Escalation and Closure

Once the messages are implemented for ticket creation, add the same for the priority updates within the updatePrioritySignal listener, by including the following within the success block:

```
self.applicationMessages.push(
        {
            severity: 'confirmation',
            summary: 'Priority increased',
            detail: 'The ticket ' + model.id + ' has had its priority
            increased to ' + newPriority
        }
)
```

Then include the following message within the error block:

```
self.applicationMessages.push(
        {
```

213

```
      severity: 'error',
      summary: 'Error updating ticket',
      detail: 'Unable to increase priority for ticket ' +
      modelData.id
    }
)
```

Next within closeTicketSignal listener, add the following into the success block:

```
self.applicationMessages.push(
        {
          severity: 'confirmation',
          summary: 'Ticket Closed',
          detail: 'The ticket ' + model.id + ' has been successfully
          closed'
        }
)
```

Also, add the following message within the error block:

```
self.applicationMessages.push(
        {
          severity: 'error',
          summary: 'Error closing ticket',
          detail: 'Unable to close ticket ' + modelData.id
        }
)
```

Navigate to and open API/mocks/tickets/__/PUT.mock and change the header response code to "404 Not Found" instead of "200 OK," as follows:

```
HTTP/1.1 404 Not Found
```

Now, when trying to close ticket 10002, an error should appear instead of a success message, as shown within Figure 12-3. Don't forget to change the header response code back to 200 afterward.

Figure 12-3. *Error message when closing a ticket*

Ticket Replies

Messages should also be set up for ticket replies, but as this functionality is within a different module from the one in which the applicationMessages array is defined, we must use a signal to inform the ticket-desk ViewModel of any activity.

First, open view-ticket.js and add the following variable for the new signal:

```
self.ticketReplyFailure = params.ticketReplyFailure
```

Next, dispatch an event within the catch block situated inside the ticketReply function, by including the following line of code:

```
self.ticketReplyFailure.dispatch();
```

Include the same line of code within the error block inside the addTicketReply ToCollection function.

215

Then, within ticket-desk.js, declare the signal and create the listener to push the new message onto the messages array:

```
self.ticketReplyFailure = new signals.Signal();

/* Ticket Reply Failure listener */
self.ticketReplyFailure.add(function () {
        self.applicationMessages.push(
          {
            severity: 'error',
            summary: 'Error replying to ticket',
            detail: 'Unable to reply to ticket, please try again.'
          }
        )
})
```

Finally, pass the new signal into the view ticket module component within the ticket-desk.html file as a parameter, as you have done previously with other signals.

Navigate to and open API/mocks/tickets/replies/__/POST.mock and change the header response code to "404 Not Found" instead of "200 OK," as follows:

```
HTTP/1.1 404 Not Found
```

Don't forget to change the header response code back to 200 after you have tested the fake error response.

Validation

Validation can often be a difficult area to get right, with larger applications having complicated validation rules that must be written. Oracle JET provides various mechanisms for handling client-side validation, from a simple required field to more complex regex validators. In this section, we are going to look into the basic validation of checking that required fields are populated and also writing our own validation check for the text editor, as, unfortunately, the text editor API does not come with any validation capabilities.

First, open the create ticket View and find the ojLabel component for the ticket title. On this label, add the `show-required` attribute and set its value to `true`. Setting this value to `true` will visually indicate to the user that the field is required, by setting an asterisk next to the label.

Next, add a `required` attribute to the ojInputText for the title and set the value of the attribute to `true`. Doing so will set the standard HTML required attribute on the input, and, implicitly, an Oracle JET validator is created.

The required attributes have now been set for the title, but we still have to run the validation when a user clicks the ticket creation button. To do this, head over to the `createTicket` function in the ViewModel and add the following code:

```
var titleInputBox = document.getElementById('title');
titleInputBox.validate();
```

The preceding code will fetch the input component and run the validate method on that component. The method will run any validations attached to the component, and in this case, it will validate that a value has been entered. It is then possible to check the `valid` attribute on the component, to see if it has passed validation. We don't want to create a ticket if the validation has failed; therefore, you should wrap the rest of the `createTicket` function in a conditional check and only run the create ticket logic if the validation has passed. For example:

```
if (titleInputBox.valid === 'valid'){
        // Your ticket creation logic should be here
}
```

There are two more fields to validate when creating a ticket: priority and issue summary. Priority is an LOV (List of Values), in which a value must be selected, so all that must be done is to set the `show-required` attribute to `true` on the label.

The other field, issue summary, is a little different. This is not an Oracle JET component, and we cannot use the JET component validation. Instead, we will create our own validation check. To do this, first set the `show-required` field on the label for the `new-ticket-area` and then, below the `new-ticket-area` element, add Listing 12-2.

Listing 12-2. Issue Summary Validation

```
<oj-bind-if test="[[messageTextEmpty]]">
        <div class="oj-messaging-inline-container">
            <div class="oj-message oj-message-error">
                <span class="oj-component-icon oj-message-status-icon
                oj-message-error-icon" title="Error" role="img"></span>
                <span class="oj-message-content">
                    <div class="oj-message-summary">Value is required.</div>
                    <div class="oj-message-detail"><span>You must enter
                    a value.</span>
                    </div>
                </span>
            </div>
        </div>
</oj-bind-if>
```

This code will replicate the look and feel of the error message that is shown when the Oracle JET components fail validation, so that it looks consistent to the user, despite the components not being JET components.

Next, create a new variable in the create ticket ViewModel, which is used to determine whether the message text is displayed.

```
self.messageTextEmpty = ko.observable(false);
```

Within the createTicket function before the validation conditional check, include the following:

```
if ($('#new-ticket-area').trumbowyg('html') === '') {
    $('#new-ticket-area').parent().addClass("trumbowyg-invalid");
    self.messageTextEmpty(true)
} else {
    self.messageTextEmpty(false)
}
```

This piece of code will check for a value within the ticket area, and if there is no value, it will set a new class on the area, to change the border to red and set the messageTextEmpty value to `true`, so that the error message is shown to the user.

If the value is empty, we should also prevent the ticket from being submitted. The conditional statement already created previously should be updated to look like the following, which checks for the empty value and, if it is not empty, will reset the messageText empty value to `false` and remove the invalid class:

```
if (titleInputBox.valid === 'valid' && !self.messageTextEmpty()) {
                self.messageTextEmpty(false)
                $('#new-ticket-area').parent().removeClass("trumbowyg-
invalid");
        // Your ticket creation logic should be here
}
```

Finally, create a new SASS partial called `_forms.scss` within the base directory and add the following classes into it. Don't forget to import the new partial within mosTheme.scss too.

```
.trumbowyg-box {
    margin:0px !important;
}
.trumbowyg-invalid {
    border: 2px solid $accentColorDanger3;
}
```

Once this has been done, you can rerun the application and see the validation in action, as shown in Figure 12-4. You should also now go and apply the trumboyg validation to the ticket reply area, as you have done previously for the ticket creation.

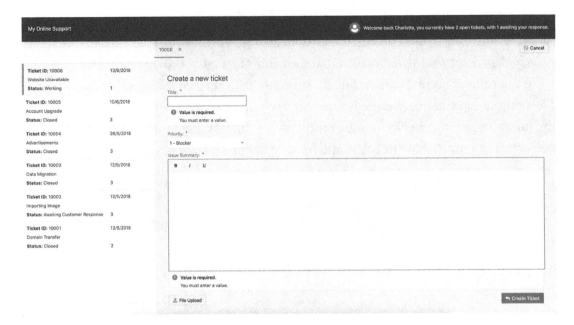

Figure 12-4. *Required field validation on ticket creation*

Summary

In this chapter, you have explored three different subjects: logging, messages, and validation. By using the built-in Oracle JET logger, you have gone back and changed any standard console logging with the JET logger and seen how you can set a default logging level for the whole application. The messages component is used to provide feedback to the user when actions are performed, in the form of success or error messages for ticket creation, closing, priority updates, and replies.

Finally, validators were attached to the input components, to check if the field has been populated, and custom validation was built for the text editor.

CHAPTER 13

Automated Unit Testing

Ah, unit testing! It takes a multitude of things coming together to ensure that a team of developers write good automated unit tests for their work. One of these things is deciding on a unit test framework to use (it's a bit of a maze out there). Another is making it really easy for developers to write their tests.

Unit testing can tend to be an afterthought, and the last thing you want to worry about when you are facing tight deadlines is having to learn a new testing framework on top of the pile of other tasks you likely have on your backlog. This chapter will walk through getting a skeleton unit test framework working in your project—ready for those important automated tests to be written. The examples in the chapter uses the Jasmine testing framework (with Karma as a test runner) within an Oracle JET project. However, you are free to use any unit testing framework you want with Oracle JET, such as QUnit.

Installing Karma and Jasmine

To begin, the necessary libraries must be installed into the project. Run the following command within the UI directory, to install the dependencies for Karma and Jasmine:

```
npm install karma karma-jasmine karma-chrome-launcher jasmine-core karma-coverage karma-requirejs
```

Next, install the Karma Command Line Interface (CLI) globally:

```
npm install -g karma-cli
```

Karma Setup

Now that the libraries are installed, we can set up the Karma configuration. There is a command (karma init) that can set up this configuration file up with wizard-like questions. However, for this example, we will create and set up the file ourselves, to better understand what it is doing.

© Daniel Curtis 2019

D. Curtis, *Practical Oracle JET*, https://doi.org/10.1007/978-1-4842-4346-6_13

Create a new file called `karma.conf.js` within the UI directory. Inside the file, there are multiple options that we should configure. Let's walk though these now, and the full code will be included just afterward.

The first option is the `basePath`, which is the initial starting point for any directory paths within the Karma runner. Leave the `basePath` as blank.

```
basePath: ''
```

Then there are the frameworks that Karma will require. We want to specify these as *Jasmine* and *RequireJS*:

```
frameworks: ['jasmine', 'requirejs']
```

When Karma runs, it will spin up web browser instances to run the tests, and the files that Karma will be loading into the browser can be set using the `files` attribute. These patterns are resolved using glob and will have the `basePath` appended to the beginning. The `included: false` attribute is required on some of the files, to prevent Karma loading them into a script tag within the browser, and, instead, they will get loaded by RequireJS.

In the following example, we are also excluding the `main.js` file, as we do not need it to run for our tests. Instead, we will shortly be creating a new `main.js` file specifically for the test runner.

```
files: [
  {pattern: 'web/js/libs/jquery/jquery-3.3.1.js'},
  {pattern: 'web/js/**/*.js', included: false},
  {pattern: 'web/js/jet-composites/**/*', included: false },
  {pattern: 'web/js/viewModels/*.js', included: false},
  {pattern: 'tests/fixtures/**/*.json', included: false},
  {pattern: 'tests/**/*-spec.js', included: false},
  'tests/test-main.js'
]
exclude: [
  'web/js/main.js'
],
```

Next, we want to set up the coverage reporting. We are going to use the karma-coverage library, which uses the Istanbul code coverage tool. Add the following preprocessor block, as well as specifying the reporters and the location to store the reports:

```
preprocessors: {
     'src/js/viewModels/*.js':['coverage']
},
reporters: ['progress','coverage'],
coverageReporter:{
     type:'html',
     dir:'reports/'
}
```

Then there are a couple more configurations to set, including port, colors (which enables or disables colors in the reporter and logs), the log level, and whether the files should be auto-watched.

```
port: 9876,
colors: true,
logLevel: config.LOG_INFO,
autoWatch: true,
```

Finally, we must specify what browsers the tests should run on. There are a bunch of different browsers and browser launchers that can be used, and it is also possible to run some of the browsers in "headless" mode. Headless mode will open and run the tests in the browser but not obstruct your work by popping open in front of your other windows. It will quietly run in the background. To run in headless mode, you should append Headless to the end of the browser name. For example, Chrome would become ChromeHeadless. I will be using the Chrome browser for my testing, but feel free to change this to your preferred browser.

```
browsers: ['Chrome'],
```

That is everything set up for the karma.conf.js file, and the full file should look like Listing 13-1.

Listing 13-1. The Full `karma.conf.js` File

```
// Karma configuration

module.exports = function(config) {
  config.set({

    // base path that will be used to resolve all patterns (eg. files, exclude)
    basePath: '',

    // frameworks to use
    // available frameworks: https://npmjs.org/browse/keyword/karma-adapter
    frameworks: ['jasmine', 'requirejs'],

    // list of files / patterns to load in the browser
    files: [
      {pattern: 'web/js/libs/jquery/jquery-3.3.1.js'},
      {pattern: 'web/js/**/*.js', included: false},
      {pattern: 'web/js/jet-composites/**/*', included: false },
      {pattern: 'web/js/viewModels/*.js', included: false},
      {pattern: 'tests/fixtures/**/*.json', included: false},
      {pattern: 'tests/**/*-spec.js', included: false},
      'tests/test-main.js'
    ],

    // list of files / patterns to exclude
    exclude: [
      'web/js/main.js'
    ],

    // preprocess matching files before serving them to the browser
    // available preprocessors: https://npmjs.org/browse/keyword/karma-
    preprocessor
    preprocessors: {
      'web/js/viewModels/*.js':['coverage']
    },
```

```
// test results reporter to use
// possible values: 'dots', 'progress'
// available reporters: https://npmjs.org/browse/keyword/karma-reporter
reporters: ['progress','coverage'],
coverageReporter:{
  type:'html',
  dir:'reports/'
},

// web server port
port: 9876,

// enable / disable colors in the output (reporters and logs)
colors: true,

// level of logging
// possible values: config.LOG_DISABLE || config.LOG_ERROR || config.
LOG_WARN || config.LOG_INFO || config.LOG_DEBUG
logLevel: config.LOG_INFO,

// enable / disable watching file and executing tests whenever any file changes
autoWatch: true,

// start these browsers
// available browser launchers: https://npmjs.org/browse/keyword/karma-launcher
browsers: ['Chrome'],

  })
}
```

test-main Setup

Now, we can move on to the test-main.js file, which is the replacement for the standard main.js file we include in the application. The test-main.js file will be responsible for finding and loading all of the ViewModels and test files within the application. (Test files must be named as the ViewModel name followed by -spec.)

Create a new folder called tests in the UI directory and create test-main.js within that new directory. Listing 13-2 shows the file for our example.

Listing 13-2. The test-main.js File

```
var TEST_REGEXP = /(spec)\.js$/i;
var VIEWMODEL_REGEXP = /viewModels\//
var allTestFiles = [];
var allModules = [];

var normalizedTestModule = function(file) {
    return file.replace(/\.js$/, '');
}

// Get a list of all the test files to include
Object.keys(window.__karma__.files).forEach(function(file) {
  if (TEST_REGEXP.test(file)) {
    allTestFiles.push(file);
  } else if(VIEWMODEL_REGEXP.test(file)){
    allModules.push(normalizedTestModule(file))
  }
});

require.config({
  // Karma serves files under /base, which is the basePath from your config file
  baseUrl: '/base/web/js',

  // example of using a couple of path translations (paths), to allow us to
  // refer to different library dependencies, without using relative paths
  paths:
    {
      knockout: 'libs/knockout/knockout-3.4.2.debug',
      jquery: 'libs/jquery/jquery-3.3.1',
      'jqueryui-amd': 'libs/jquery/jqueryui-amd-1.12.1',
      promise: 'libs/es6-promise/es6-promise',
      hammerjs: 'libs/hammer/hammer-2.0.8',
      ojdnd: 'libs/dnd-polyfill/dnd-polyfill-1.0.0',
      ojs: 'libs/oj/v6.0.0/debug',
```

```
      ojL10n: 'libs/oj/v6.0.0/ojL10n',
      ojtranslations: 'libs/oj/v6.0.0/resources',
      text: 'libs/require/text',
      signals: 'libs/js-signals/signals',
      customElements: 'libs/webcomponents/custom-elements.min',
      css: 'libs/require-css/css',
      appUtils: 'utils/appUtils',
      Dragibility: 'libs/draggability/draggabilly.pkgd',
      bridget: 'libs/bridget/jquery-bridget',
      'touchr': 'libs/touchr/touchr',
      'trumbowyg': 'libs/trumbowyg/trumbowyg.min',
      'appUtils': 'utils/app-utils',
      'inline-search': 'jet-composites/inline-search/1.0.0'
      },

  // example of using a shim, to load non AMD libraries (such as underscore)
  shim:
  {'jquery':
    {
      exports: ['jQuery', '$']
    }
  },

  // dynamically load all test files
  deps: allTestFiles,

  // we have to kickoff jasmine, as it is asynchronous
  callback: require(allModules, function () {
    window.__karma__.start()
  })
});
```

Try running karma start within a new terminal window in the UI directory, to check that everything is running. Chrome should open a new browser window and show results similar to those in Figure 13-1.

Figure 13-1. *Karma successfully running*

Writing a Test

With the framework in place, it is now possible to start writing tests. To create your first test, add a new file called ticket-desk-spec.js within the UI/tests directory. Inside the new file, add the following code shown in Listing 13-3:

Listing 13-3. The ticket-desk-spec.js File

```
define(['viewModels/ticket-desk'], function (TicketDeskViewModel) {
    describe('Ticket Desk Module - ', function () {
        var viewModel;
        beforeEach(function () {
            viewModel = new TicketDeskViewModel();
        });

        describe('Example Test for onTabRemove Function - ', function () {
            it('Check onTabRemove function runs and passes the tab ID to
            the delete tab function', function () {
                const deleteTabSpy = spyOn(viewModel, 'deleteTab');
                const event = {
                    detail: {
                        key: 1
                    },
                    preventDefault() { },
```

```
              stopPropagation() { }
          }

          viewModel.onTabRemove(event);
          expect(deleteTabSpy).toHaveBeenCalledWith(1);
        });
      });
    });
});
```

This is a really simple test for the onTabRemove function with `ticket-desk.js`. The code begins by loading the `ticket-desk` ViewModel within the `define` block, so that we can run tests against it. The ViewModel instance is initialized before each test from within the `beforeEach` function. The `it` block sets up a new test to check whether the `deleteTab` method is called from within the `onTabRemove` function, with the correct ID passed into it.

To run the tests, make sure the Karma CLI is still running and that the application is running too. When the files are changed, the Karma CLI should automatically detect changes. All being well, you should receive a success message in the Karma CLI and changing the key value in the event object to another number should fail the test.

When you begin to write more tests for your application, the reports are generated and stored within the `UI/reports` directory. These reports will give a breakdown of code coverage per ViewModel.

Figure 13-2 shows an overall coverage percentage for all the ViewModels.

File ▲		Statements	
create-ticket.js		8.11%	3/37
ticket-desk.js		41.24%	40/97
view-representative.js		18.75%	3/16
view-ticket.js		2.78%	3/108

Figure 13-2. *Overall coverage statistics for all ViewModels*

Figure 13-3 shows the functions within a ViewModel that have been covered by the tests. In this figure, you can see that `onTabRemove` has been covered by our preceding test, but the `tabSelectionChanged` function has not yet been tested.

```
1×        self.onTabRemove = function (event) {
1×          self.deleteTab(event.detail.key);
1×          event.preventDefault();
1×          event.stopPropagation();
          };

1×        self.tabSelectionChanged = function () {
            if(self.ticketList().get(self.selectedTabItem()) === undefined){
              document.getElementById("search-component").resetSearch();
            }

            oj.Context.getContext(document.getElementById("search-component"))
              .getBusyContext()
              .whenReady()
              .then(function () {
                self.selectedTicketModel(self.ticketList().get(self.selectedTabItem()))
                self.selectedTicket([self.selectedTabItem()])
              })
          }
```

Figure 13-3. *Code-level coverage report for* `ticket-desk.js`

Summary

In this, the final chapter of *Practical Oracle JET*, you have explored Jasmine and Karma. You have installed the relevant libraries and set the confirmation of Jasmine and Karma to support a JET application. Finally, you have created your first simple test and should now be in a position to write further tests for the application.

Index

A

add method, 163
addTicketReplytoCollection function,
153–154
Animation, 193–194
animationsUtils method, 194
Application structure, set up
avatar component, 103
dashboard module files, 92
list component in view, 94–95
list ViewModel, creation, 96–98
ojModule component, 94
tab View, creation, 99–102
ticket-desk.html file, 93
Asynchronous module definition (AMD), 8
Automatic dependency propagation
KnockoutJS, 17
ko.observable function, 17

B

Backbone JS, JET
JSFiddle workspace, 25
models and collections, 24
RequireJS configuration, 26–27
template, creation, 29–30
ViewModel function, 27–28
beforeEach function, 229
Browser logging, 209
error message, 210

err parameter, 210
general message, 210
information message, 210
levels, 210
ojLogger, 211
testing and debugging, 209
warning message, 210
Built-in hook points, 57
bytesToSize function, 206

C

Callback function, 145, 150, 164
Closed source usability, 4
Close ticket confirmation
mock-up, 41–42
Closure confirmation dialog, 167
Cloud computing, 4
Command Line Interface (CLI), 50
Container height, 104–105
copyCustomLibsToStaging
object, 56, 156
create-ticket.html file, 194
createVisible variable, 192
customURL attribute, 154

D

Declarative bindings
attributes, 18
CSS classes, 18

CPSIA information can be obtained
at www.ICGtesting.com
Printed in the USA
BVHW010217230519
549112BV00007B/132/P